Praise f

"In ManifestHer, Stef urges us all to get in touch with
what we really desire and finally live a life that moves us in the direction of our
biggest dreams surrounded with like-minded people who lift us up. Any dream
is welcome, but staying stuck and not moving toward that dream is no longer a
choice."
—Lori Harder, best-selling author of *A Tribe Called Bliss*

"ManifestHer is an actionable guide to goal setting and goal getting. If you are
feeling stuck and you want to get unstuck, start here. If you are feeling lost and
not sure how to find your way, start here. This book will guide you from doubting
your dreams to actually living them."
—Amber Rae, best-selling author of *Choose Wonder Over Worry*

"In this book, Stef offers a step-by-step guide to navigating the ambiguity
of what comes after your prescribed life comes to an end. She combines her
experiences, her knowledge, and the tools that have helped her into a practical
guide that is guaranteed to inspire you to get unstuck, navigate the ambiguity of
your post-prescribed life, and manifest your biggest dreams."
**—Lauren Doyle, Two-Time Rugby World Cup Gold Medalist and Captain, Team
USA Women's Rugby**

"ManifestHer is the wake-up call you need to step into your own badassness. It
dissolves the feelings of fear that hold you back from being in action. You gain
confidence, form deeper personal connections and friendships, and step into the
highest version of yourself. You learn to love yourself, believe in yourself, and take
your life to the next level.
—Lindsey Kaalberg, CEO and Founder, Ritual Hot Yoga

"What's the difference between a Wantrepreneur and an Entrepreneur? One month. In one month, the Wantrepreneur has an idea but the Entrepreneur has a plan and is acting on that plan. ManifestHer will make you uncomfortable. It will make you question whether you are the metaphorical equivalent of an Entrepreneur or a Wantrepreneur. It will force you to question what you've been doing so far and inspire you to take action. It will force you to ask yourself, 'Am I willing?' Read this if you are done making excuses. Read this if you are ready to take action. Read this if you are ready to seriously level up."

—Angie Nuno, CEO and Founder, Fit Bitch Lifestyle

"ManifestHer changed the way I view creating deep-rooted relationships and getting comfortable with being uncomfortable. It stripped me of my emotional walls. Forced me to confess my fears and biggest dreams. Most important, ManifestHer helped me reveal scars that have been holding me back from moving forward. This is how dreams are born. ManifestHer gives you the tools to pave the path to achieve them! Stef's ability to raise people up and make them feel powerful is truly a gift."

—Gabby Dallecarbonare, ManifestHer

Manifest
HER

^
signed By me+
my Bestie! Ck gold
medalist!

FOREWORD BY LAUREN DOYLE
TEAM USA RUGBY GOLD MEDALIST

Manifest HER

THE AMBITIOUS WOMAN'S GUIDE TO: GETTING UNSTUCK, NAVIGATING THE AMBIGUITY OF YOUR POST-PRESCRIBED LIFE, AND MANIFESTING YOUR BIGGEST DREAMS

STEF CALDWELL

This is for you.

To my mom, dad, brothers, grandmothers, husband, the Commune, Cooper, my business partners, mentors, friends, expanders, and all of our current and future ManifestHers. Thank you for your unwavering support in moving the Manifest mission forward by creating space at the table for ambitious women to authentically connect (not compete) and move forward, together.

And to you, yes, you, ManifestHer reading this book—this is for you. Thank you for being part of this terrific journey and allowing me to have even the smallest influence on yours. I hope the tools in this book inspire you to step into the woman you were born to be, to step confidently into your future, into your ManifestHer.

Your Guide

to ManifestHer

Foreword

WHEN YOU GET THE HONOR of knowing someone as not only a friend but a teammate and roommate as well, you truly experience all sides of that person. There is no hiding your true colors when you spend nearly every single hour of your existence together.

I met Stef ten years ago at Eastern Illinois University where we played rugby together, lived together, and became tremendous friends. There are people that come into your life and they are meant to be main characters on your journey. Stef is one of those people for me.

Her energy is magnetic and she has a way of owning every room she walks into. Her warmth radiates to all of those who she cares deeply about, and her ability to turn ideas into action is something that inspires everyone in her orbit. More than anything, her endurance, her tirelessness, and her capacity to set and achieve goals and outwork anyone is something I think everyone can learn from.

I first witnessed her capacity to outwork everyone around her during her sophomore season on the team where, after an average freshman season, Stef left for the summer and came back thirty pounds lighter with the fastest mile time on the team. Her fitness led her to a new position on the field where she broke tackle records and kept up with me, ensuring that when I went down in a tackle, she was there to protect me. That year, she was awarded the Most Improved Player award.

As captain of USA Rugby and a two-time HSBC World Series champion, I get the opportunity to play alongside and against the best caliber talent in the world, and if there is one thing I've learned on my journey, it's that hard work beats natural talent every time. The best players in the world have a relentless focus on hard work. They put in the hours while everyone else is asleep, and when they show up on game day, they execute.

I've had the honor of watching Stef take on *the real world* the same way she took on rugby, navigating the ambiguity of her post-prescribed life with fearlessness and educating all of us in the wake of her experiences both good and bad. Stef is like a heat-seeking missile for all things she wants to accomplish in life. When she says she wants to do something, you can consider it done.

When we were graduating college, Stef said she wanted to move to Chicago, make a six-figure salary, and run her own company by the age of thirty. When Stef was twenty-seven, she had accomplished every one of those goals.

A year ago, Stef said she was stuck and wanted to get unstuck, and Manifest was born.

A year ago, Stef said she wanted to help women connect and move forward together. Manifest has impacted hundreds of women, some of whom say that attending ManifestHer changed their lives—they went back to college, they got promotions, they left relationships, they took action on their biggest dreams.

A year ago, Stef said she wanted to write a book, and here it is.

She is living proof that if you can dream it, and if you are willing to put in the work to achieve it, you can manifest it into your reality. She is living proof that when you move through the world with good intentions, when you have a clear destination, and when you take action every single day, whatever you want to accomplish is yours for the taking.

In this book, Stef offers a step-by-step guide to navigating the ambiguity of what comes after your prescribed life comes to an end. She combines her experiences, her knowledge, and the tools that have helped her into a practical guide that is guaranteed to inspire you to get unstuck, navigate the ambiguity of your post-prescribed life, and manifest your biggest dreams.

I've had the privilege of being inspired by and mentored by Stef for the last ten years, and I couldn't be more excited that through this book she is sharing her experiences and the knowledge and tools she's collected along the way to help more women manifest their biggest dreams.

Lauren Doyle, Captain, Team USA Women's Rugby, and Two-Time HSBC Rugby World Series Gold Medalist

Dear ManifestHer,

I see you there, standing there at the trailhead of your potential. I can see how badly you want to step onto the path, but you are paralyzed by fear and uncertainty because what comes next is uncharted territory. There's no map for what comes after you finish your formal education, or what I call your prescribed life, and so you are lost in the sea of ambiguity of your post-prescribed life.

Congrats, by the way. You finished school (at whatever level was meant for you) and you've managed to land a job that's paying the bills, but you thought by the time you had accomplished all this, someone—anyone—would hand you a complete guide for navigating the rest of your life.

You fear stagnating. You fear the unknown. You fear saying you want something, going after it, and failing. You aren't sure what you fear more, stagnating or self-inflicted change. Why? Because change means uncertainty, and when you can't be certain, you are certain that the outcome *could* be bad.

But there's a voice inside you that whispers to you at night "You are meant for more," and you've been trying to drown her out because even though you know you are meant for more, you are not sure what that *more* is, and that scares you. You've been waiting for a sign or a permission slip but it hasn't come yet and so you are starting to feel like Bill Murray in *Groundhog Day*: wake, work, sleep, repeat.

And this scares you, because it is scary to feel like you don't know what your purpose is, but the only thing that scares you more than not knowing your purpose is not ever figuring it out and letting your entire life slip by without realizing your potential and fulfilling your purpose.

You are ambitious. You are resourceful. You've been told you are a creative problem solver. You have incredible drive and dedication.

At the same time, you struggle with your anxiety; you struggle to trust that these "strengths" you've been told you possess are *actually* your strengths. To some extent, you feel that you've been lied to your whole life. You've managed to convince yourself that you are not enough to be at the table you were invited to, and that makes it impossible for you to stay focused on your strengths because you have this ongoing inner chatter that reminds you every day, "You are running out of time." This gives you even more anxiety because, well, you *are* running out of time, but time for *what exactly*? You still don't know, because you don't know what your purpose is and even if you did, you wouldn't know how to pursue it.

What you are looking for more than anything is someone to help, someone to connect with, someone to share this with, someone who doesn't want to compete with you, someone who you can authentically open up to and be real with and talk about these things with. You are starting to realize maybe the permission slip and the map you so desperately want is never coming and if it's not coming, you need a new plan for moving forward.

Sound familiar? Yeah, me too.

xo,

Stef

The Problem

YOU FINISHED SCHOOL, GOT YOUR JOB, and now everyday is Groundhog Day. You look forward to the weekend because it's the only chance you get to break up the noise between your routine of sleep, wake, work, repeat.

The only way to describe what you feel right now is "stuck." You feel like you are on a hamster wheel and can't get off.

You know you were born for more, but you can't exactly describe what *more* would look like.

You used to have big dreams for your life—big, beautiful, extraordinary dreams. But now you struggle to dream of what life could be like in one year, not to mention ten years.

You've got limited free time, you've got debt, and you feel like these practical matters are preventing you from pursuing a life bigger than the one you are leading.

But something's gotta give because you can't go on like this forever.

You want to get unstuck and manifest *her*.

Who is this ManifestHer?

She is you, the *you* that you were born to be.

The Solution

YOU KNOW *EXACTLY* WHAT THE SOLUTION IS.

A definitive guide for navigating the sea of ambiguity, through the straits of certainty, to the promised land of your potential and how to thrive on your journey there.

You picked up this book because everything I just said resonated with you and *you want this book to be the solution*, the definitive guide for navigating the ambiguity of your post-prescribed life.

So will it be? I don't know. That's up to you to decide.

Why

YOU WOULD KEEP READING THIS BOOK

MY NAME IS STEF, I am twenty-nine, and I am the founder of Manifest, in addition to being a full-timer working in high tech at an incredible and innovative AI company in Chicago.

At Manifest, our mission is to create the most badass community of women *ever*, a community of women who support each other's ambitions and challenge each other to take action—a community of women who empower each other through our collective knowledge and networks and encourage each other to realize our own and collective potential.

We do this by curating experiences that facilitate authentic connection and accountability between ambitious women. Everything I said in the above section came directly from the women of our community, women who sit at our table and pour into us their biggest dreams, their biggest fears, all the reasons why they hold themselves back, and all the plans they have to stop doing that and to start taking action when they leave our table.

These women are just like you: future entrepreneurs, future executives, future doctors, future authors, future influencers, future mamas, future philanthropists, movers, shakers, game-changers and more.

And now, these women are leveraging the tools we share in this book to take action toward realizing their potential and fulfilling their purpose, to ManifestHer.

At one point, all of the women in our community (including me) felt stuck, but by using these tools and each other, we've managed to get unstuck and to navigate uncertainty in the direction of our ever-evolving ambitions and in pursuit of realizing our potential and fulfilling our purpose.

The stories and tools in this book will help you identify and disrupt the limiting beliefs you hold about yourself, your relationships with others, and about your life. It will help you revisit those big dreams you once had and recalibrate and bring structure to what those dreams are today. It will challenge you to take action toward achieving those dreams through a practical lens and help you build a more productive relationship with yourself, others, and the universe on your journey.

I'm eternally grateful you picked up this book, and I promise to provide you with a curriculum that will empower you to become unstuck and to confidently navigate the ambiguity of your post-prescribed life and start manifesting your biggest dreams.

But before we go on this journey together, I think you and I need to make our own personal connection so you can know where I'm coming from and trust in me that I have your best intentions at heart and that more than anything, I want to support you and see you succeed. I'm a little nervous to tell you all of this, so just promise me, if I share my truth, you'll share yours.

About Me . . .

"I AM NOT ENOUGH"
WHEN I WAS SIXTEEN, I COMMITTED SUICIDE.

Fortunately, I failed.

Though at the time, I did not feel that way.

Less than one year later and completely by chance, I witnessed a man set himself ablaze in a public parking lot and despite trying to save him, he succeeded in ending his own life.

Sixteen was a hard year for me. I had incredibly low self-worth despite having an upbringing filled with love.

I grew up in a beautiful home with two successful, self-made, upper middle class parents and two hard-charging brothers. People who knew me at the time would have told you I was pretty, smart, funny. I was an honors student, an athlete, and a social chameleon navigating and charming the likes of the cool kids, the jocks, the bookworms, and the theater kids with ease.

What they didn't know was that I was battling an inner dialogue that I couldn't shut up, and she played like a broken record in my head every day. "You are not enough," she repeated to me over, and over, and over.

"You are not pretty enough," she said as I navigated the first romantic relationships of my life. "You are not fast enough," she said, as I ran up and down the court. "You are not smart enough," she said as I turned in my countless exams. "You will never be enough," she promised me as I swallowed the last of the pills and lay down, closed my eyes, and prayed to end my life, prayed I would never wake up.

"You are not even good enough to do this," she said as I woke up seizing and getting violently ill and was brought to the nearest emergency room to be revived.

My failed suicide attempt was the front bookend of the worst year of my life. The back bookend was when I witnessed a man succeed in doing what I had so badly wanted for myself.

When I woke up from the trauma of the experience of seeing a man literally set himself and his life ablaze, it was as if my negative inner dialogue had moved out and was replaced by a more positive one. "His fate will not be your fate," she said to me. "You are meant for more," she promised me, just in time for me to accept a scholarship to play Women's Rugby for the premiere NCAA Division 1 team in the United States of America and to move my life to Charleston, Illinois, where I would spend the next four years discovering who I was and what I wanted for my life.

"I AM UNSTOPPABLE"

College had its challenges, but none as bad as high school. Sure, there were days when I questioned my ability to perform intellectually, socially, on the field, in the weight room.

And yes, there were moments when I compared myself to my teammates, my classmates, my sorority sisters and felt I had come up with the short end of the stick, but all in all, my soul was happy and my mind fed me more productive narratives about myself and my worth.

By my junior year, I had worked my way into leadership positions on and off the field. I was honored with the Most Improved Player award, I lost thirty pounds, and had the fastest mile time on the team. I was vice president of recruitment for my sorority, I was president of the American Marketing Association, and on top of all of this, I had a nearly perfect GPA and was a model member of the university's honors program.

When my rugby coach asked me to lead an initiative to help our team raise money and awareness, I came up with the idea to create a line of T-shirts with empowering phrases written in bold letters across the front of them in a variety of colors.

"I Am Fearless" read one. "I Am Powerful" read another.

"I Am Unstoppable" read mine. And when I wore it, I felt it. There was nothing I couldn't accomplish, I was certain of it: *I. Am. Unstoppable.*

As my college experience neared completion, I found myself overcome with anxiety. I knew who I was here. I was finally hitting my stride. I felt worthy here. I felt enough here. Every step forward in my life had been prescribed up until this point. What would life be like after college? What steps were next? What would I do with no one to tell me what to do?

It was at this crucial moment in my life that I received a gift from the universe: my very first piece of Lululemon gear.

Okay, it was actually from my then boyfriend, now husband, but that's beside the point. Regardless, it was a beautiful purple zip-up that spoke to my soul in a way that only Lululemon clothing can. I had never heard of the brand when Ronnie gave me the gift, but he told me it was one of the trendiest fitness brands in Chicago, and I had to learn more.

As any good millennial would, I took to Google to discover more about this amazing company. I found their website, and it did not disappoint. An entire section of their site is dedicated to helping people set and achieve goals, complete with video courses and printouts to help you define your vision for your life and create an action plan to achieve that vision.

Timing is everything, and I knew this was *the* gift from the universe I had been waiting for to rid myself of the anxiety I was feeling, to create a prescription for myself to thrive in my inevitable and impending post-prescribed life.

The Lululemon Goal Setting Program encourages people to set goals on a ten-year horizon. The reason for this particular length of time is that over such a long horizon, you are more capable of taking the excuses of time, money, and knowledge off the table for yourself. Therefore, you feel more confident to dream big and know that if you work hard, you can actually accomplish massive goals. The program also suggests you should define goals across three different dimensions of your life—your professional goals, your personal goals, and your health goals—and write them in the present tense. For example, "In ten years, I am . . ."

I was twenty-two years old, and I sat down to spend hours thinking about what I wanted to accomplish in my personal, professional, and health life over the next ten years—so, by age thirty-two.

"In ten years, I am making a six-figure salary and working for a company I love whose mission motivates me."

"In ten years, I am married and living in a beautiful home with a man I love."

"In ten years, I am healthy and fit and I have completed a marathon."

When graduation day came around, I confidently accepted my diploma knowing that whatever came next, I was prepared. I had a self-prescribed guide for what came next and was ready for the next chapter of my life.

"NO, YOU ARE ACTUALLY QUITE STOPPABLE"

Fast-forward five years from college graduation, and I am twenty-seven. I am engaged to the man I love, living in a beautiful apartment in Chicago with a beautiful second home in southwest Michigan, one block off of Lake Michigan. Together, we have the most adorable Pomeranian named Cooper, and I have successfully completed the Chicago Marathon.

I am making six-figures and working my dream job for, objectively speaking, one of the most innovative AI companies in the world, calling on executives from some of the most interesting technology companies in the world.

Life is good, and I am deeply proud of having achieved every single one of my ten-year goals, reaching my personal summit five years ahead of plan, and then my phone rings.

"We're dissolving the business development team," my boss informs me, and my world came to a screeching halt.

Cue: devastation.

This was my dream job, which I had managed to procure at the ripe young age of twenty-seven, and with this change, I would be moving onto a new team starting the following day, doing something entirely different—and my new manager? TBD.

The next day, I stopped in my boss's office to discuss the changes coming. He recommended I apply for the open role to lead the new team where I was being moved, which would be a promotion to the next level up from my current role. "They're looking for the right person to lead the team," he suggested.

I gawked at him. I didn't meet the requirements for the role—how could I apply?

With confidence, he looked me in the eyes and said, "If there is anything I know for sure, it is that given the opportunity, you will rise to the occasion."

With his unwavering confidence in me, I decided to put my name in the hat for the role.

I prepared my ass off for the interview, spending weeks developing a perspective on how I would be the right person, with the right ideas, to mobilize and inspire a team of people to be successful in hitting some aggressive targets. I interviewed and I felt confident that if there was someone who could support this new team, it was me. I wasn't the safe choice, but I was the right choice.

I remember exactly how it felt walking into the hiring manager's office the day the decision was made and learning that despite my best efforts, I was not enough, and the team had decided to go in a different direction.

Cue: more devastation.

I had given it my best. My best was not enough. I was not enough.

I had been putting in sixty-hour weeks for two years, I had been told that I was a top performer in the company, I thought the skills and energy I brought to the table was what the company needed, and yet I was not enough and they were going in a different direction.

I couldn't keep myself together. I left the office early that day, and as I stepped out the front door of my office building, tears fell from my eyes. I did my best to choke them back as I dragged my feet the mile and a half from my office building to my apartment, trying to channel every tool I had ever come across in a self-help book to just make it home.

"Did you get it?" Ronnie asked as I stepped through the front door of our apartment.

I couldn't hold it in one more second. I burst into tears and toppled over into his arms.

"It's okay to cry about it," he told me.

We both knew it—my identity had become my work, and all of my self-worth was tied directly to my performance at the office. Just days ago, my performance with this company had confirmed my self-worth, my enoughness, my ability to succeed and thrive. Now that was in question, and I wasn't sure who I was or what was in store for my future.

I was embarrassed that I had reached for something I wanted and failed. I was embarrassed that I thought for a second that I had it in me to do the job in the first place. I was ashamed I ever thought I was worthy of this role or enough to take it on.

The jig is up. They've found me out, and now I'll have to go, I thought.

"YOU ARE MEANT FOR MORE"

And I would have gone, too, had it not been for the impeccable timing of this organizational change, just three months before our wedding. So, rather than be irrational and quit my job, I decided I would stay until after the wedding and if at that point, I still felt the way I did, I would leave my job and find a new place to work.

But, the universe had another plan, and it was during the months and the year that followed that I unlocked the next-order version of myself, the version that whispered to me, "Remember, Stef, you are meant for more," and so that is where we will start this book and this journey together.

In this book, I will share how in one calendar year, I managed to unstick myself, start a company that helped more than one hundred women unstick themselves, and get a "book deal" (more on this later) to share these ideas for getting unstuck with women like you. I will also share how I did all of this while not just working for the company that I mentioned above but performing so well that I advocated for and received promotion and a raise. And how you can do it too.

How

TO USE THIS BOOK

FOR A LONG TIME, EVEN WHILE writing this book, I thought to myself, *Who am I to write a book about this?* I always imagined that one day, when I had "made it," then I would sit down and write a book, something that was tried and true and unarguable because of the massive success I had to back me up. But then my best friend and Manifest co-founder, Tasha, reminded me that if I waited until the end of my career, I wouldn't remember what it was like at the beginning and anything I wrote then would miss the mark for those who would need it most and who need it now.

There are tons of books out there by people who have already made it; there are far fewer for people who are "in the thick of it." So I thought, *Maybe this book would be relevant for a certain group of women now, and if I delivered it to those women now, they would be able to leverage some of the experiences and knowledge I've accumulated and used to help others to help themselves!*

This book is designed to be a practical and actionable peer-to-peer guide for getting unstuck and moving in the direction of realizing your potential and fulfilling your purpose. It is to prove to you that you don't have to quit your job, run away from your life, and completely disconnect from all of your relationships and your loved ones to find yourself or your purpose. You have everything you need right now to get unstuck, get clear on your purpose, and start taking action toward realizing your potential and manifesting your biggest dreams.

This book is a step-by-step guide you can come back to time after time to remind yourself that you are enough and you are worthy and you can have the extraordinary life you know you were made for. In each chapter, I will share a personal story and the tools that helped me through that experience. At the end of each chapter, I will challenge you to reflect on the lessons in that chapter by asking you some of the same questions I had to ask myself. Finally, I will share my recommendation for your continued reading so you can continue your journey and a song to celebrate your completion of another chapter with a little dance party and inspire you to keep moving forward. If you read this book in its entirety and you actually do the challenges at the end of each chapter, you will get unstuck, you will get clear on your goals, you will take action toward those goals, and you will start manifesting your biggest dreams.

It's just that simple, but you have to do the work.

So, if you are feeling stuck and looking to get unstuck and to take action in the direction of realizing your potential and fulfilling your purpose—but under the pretense of practicality—this book is for you. If you are still wondering how to use this book, the answer is simple: actually read the chapters, actually do the challenges, and then actually do the things *in real life*.

Wishing you the best on your journey—the ball is in your court now.

Step 1

FORGIVE YOURSELF

The truth is unless you let go, unless you forgive yourself, unless you forgive the situation, unless you realize that the situation is over, you cannot move forward.
—Steve Maraboli

ACCORDING TO GALLUP'S *2017 State of the American Workplace* report,[1] over 85 percent of the workforce is not engaged or actively disengaged at work. So it's no surprise that according to another study, more than half of Americans claim they are stuck in a rut and over three quarters of people are frustrated with their progress in life.[2]

All of this research is largely consistent with what we hear from ManifestHers. They are drained by their work and their relationships and are struggling to feel like they know what their purpose is in life. Work pays the bills and they lack financial

---

1 Gallup, *State of the American Workplace*, 2013, https://www.gallup.com/workplace/238085/state-american-workplace-report-2017.aspx.
2 Don Ames, "Most Americans 'Stuck in a Rut' and Disappointed with Life," WWL Radio, August 23, 2018, https://wwl.radio.com/articles/survey-says-more-half-americans-feel-they-are-stuck-rut.

stability, so quitting is not an option. But while work takes care of the bills, it also takes a lot of their time—time they could otherwise use to get clear on their purpose, chart a clear path forward, and start taking action. This frustrates them because it makes them feel like they don't have a choice. It makes them feel like they have to live a linear life, stay stuck, pay off those bills, and live later. But "later" feels like light-years away, so completely out of reach that it makes them want to cry when they think about it.

Does this sound at all familiar? Yeah, me too.

YOU ARE FEELING STUCK

Stuck. That's how I felt the day after I found out I was not getting the promotion.

I spent the next few weeks monopolizing dinner table conversations with my girlfriends and anyone else who would listen, unloading my unhappiness on them so I didn't have to carry it all around on my own shoulders.

I had my dream job ripped from me and it was replaced with a job that I never in a million years would have picked for myself. The promotion would have been a nice consolation prize, but I was not the right candidate for that position.

Some of the feedback I had been given in the wake of the situation was that although I had presented some strong ideas as part of my interviewing process, it was clear I lacked confidence in myself and my abilities.

I had succeeded in most other things I'd ever tried to accomplish. I'd confidently navigated and sold to some of the world's most innovative executive teams. I'd given speeches and keynotes to rooms filled with hundreds and in some cases thousands of people often two to three times my age. I'd done stand up comedy and slayed, for chrissakes—how is it possible that I wasn't confident enough?

That feedback tore me apart. *Not confident enough?* It made me question how the outcome would have been different if I *had been* confident enough.

Would I have gotten the promotion if I were more confident? Would I still be feeling stuck if I had received the promotion? Was my stuckness contingent on the extrinsic feedback that called into question something intrinsically I thought I had locked in? How was this intrinsic confusion coupled with the extrinsic reality of my new job impacting me so fucking much?

These questions swirled uncontrollably in my head, causing me to go into negative spirals, doubting myself, doubting my abilities, causing me to fear raising my hand or speaking up in meetings. I wasn't myself. I didn't know who I was.

In the weeks following the news, an executive at my company stopped me after one of the worst meetings of my life and asked me if I was okay. "You seem like you are back on your heels right now," he said.

Fuuuck. People were noticing.

Just a few weeks ago, I had my shit together, I thought. *What the hell is going on with me?*

YOU ARE NOT ALONE

As it turns out, this type of feedback is commonplace for young women in the workforce, as are the negative spirals of self-doubt they cause.

Sadly, this is something that holds back women in the workforce. Even more unfortunate is that as women are held back and their male counterparts move past them, fewer women make it to middle management; thus, fewer women make it to the executive office, and even fewer women make it to the board. This lack of representation at higher levels perpetuates the situation in two ways:

First, the lack of representation of women means there are very few advocates for future generations of women in the executive office who could advocate for and implement programs to help women grow their skills and confidence so they would be in a better position to receive these promotions in the future, growing the pool of women in middle management, upper management, and ultimately the executive office and board.

Second, the limited representation of women means there are very few women mentors for young, ambitious women to seek same-gender guidance from. So while young men have same-gender mentors in such abundance that they can easily find one, two, five, ten mentors to turn to as a personal board of directors for navigating the ambiguity of their careers as individual contributors, middle management all the way to the executive office, women are lucky if they can find one, maybe two time-strapped, multi-hyphenate, badass-executives and badass-executive-mamas to grab a coffee with once a year!

The impact: Well, according to research by Katty Kay and Claire Shipman for their book *The Confidence Code: The*

Science and Art of Self-Assurance—What Women Should Know, "Compared with men, women don't consider themselves as ready for promotions, they predict they'll do worse on tests, and they generally underestimate their abilities. This disparity stems from factors ranging from upbringing to biology."[3]

And when they do muster up enough confidence to reach for the promotion and fail, it sends them into a downward spiral of self-doubt because the propensity to ruminate is much stronger in women than in their male counterparts.

> Simply put, a woman's brain is not her friend when it comes to confidence. We think too much and we think about the wrong things. Thinking harder and harder and harder won't solve our issues, though, it won't make us more confident, and it most certainly freezes decision making, not to mention action. Ruminating drains the confidence from us. Those negative thoughts, and nightmare scenarios masquerading as problem solving, spin on an endless loop. We render ourselves unable to be in the moment or to trust our instincts because we are captive to those distracting, destructive thoughts, which gradually squeeze all the spontaneity out of life and work.
>
> **—Katty Kay, *The Confidence Code: The Science and Art of Self-Assurance—What Women Should Know*[4]**

---

3 Katty Kay and Claire Shipman, "The Confidence Gap," *Atlantic*, May 2014, https://www.theatlantic.com/magazine/archive/2014/05/the-confidence-gap/359815/.
4 "Katty Kay Quotes," Goodreads, accessed December 27, 2019, https://www.goodreads.com/author/quotes/2778930.Katty_Kay.

The outcome is treacherous, and it holds women back:

What a vicious circle: girls lose confidence, so they quit competing, thereby depriving themselves of one of the best ways to regain it. They leave school crammed full of interesting historical facts and elegant Spanish subjunctives, proud of their ability to study hard and get the best grades, and determined to please. But somewhere between the classroom and the cubicle, the rules change, and they don't realize it. They slam into a work world that doesn't reward them for perfect spelling and exquisite manners. The requirements for adult success are different, and their confidence takes a beating.[5]

And unfortunately for women, the end result of all of this is that they are unable to grow their careers. They report feeling like they are stuck in a rut, disengaged at work, and frustrated with their progress in life.

After diving headfirst into this research and realizing the obstacles that plague women, I knew I had to make a choice, I could continue to play the victim, to blame the world for making me feel this way. Or I could take it upon myself to be the change I want to see in the world, to create more awareness for this issue, and to do everything in my power to create a better future for the women who were coming up with me and who would come after me.

---

[5] Katty Kay and Claire Shipman, "The Confidence Gap," *Atlantic*, May 2014, https://www.theatlantic.com/magazine/archive/2014/05/the-confi-dence-gap/359815/.

FORGIVE YOURSELF FOR FEELING STUCK

In order to move forward, we have to forgive ourselves, we have to forgive our situation, and we have to own the fact that while we can't go back and change the past, we can own and choose our futures.

I know—it's really hard to sit there and just forgive yourself, but without this *complete forgiveness*, we actually continue to hold ourselves back. When we ruminate on the past in our heads, we are actually living in the past and holding onto that regret; trying to undo the past and undo what *is* only causes us to stay stuck.

According to Sally Helgesen and Marshall Goldsmith in their book *How Women Rise*, ruminating is one of the twelve reasons women actually hold themselves back from their next raise, promotion, or job because it functions like an addiction and expends precious energy rewriting events instead of accepting them and moving on.

This is the one leap of faith we have to take together: we have to decide completely and wholly to draw a line in the sand and look at life from this point forward as everything that happened before and everything that happens after this magical moment of forgiveness.

WHAT I DID

I knew that my feeling of stuckness could be directly attributed to my not getting the promotion and the feedback that I was not confident calling into question something that I thought I knew about myself.

This confusion caused me to fall into a negative downward spiral of rumination that kept me living in the past, reliving moments where I failed to express myself confidently, and reliving moments that caused me to question my abilities. If I were ever going to move on, I needed to forgive myself completely for my past and stop reliving it in my head.

I had been contemplating quitting for weeks, and as I closed the cover on *The Confidence Code*, I made a deliberate decision to not quit. Quitting would perpetuate the issue, and what got women here won't get us where we want to go. I wanted to be part of the solution, not part of the issue.

My *Challenge* to You

What specifically has you feeling stuck?
What are the ways in which this feeling of stuckness causes you to ruminate?
How is this ruminating holding you back?
What opportunities do you have to forgive yourself
for feeling this way?
What opportunities do you have to take ownership
over your future and affect positive change for
yourself (and maybe even others)?

 Suggested *Reading*

*The Confidence Code: The Science and Art of Self-
Assurance—What Women Should Know* by Katty Kay
and Claire Shipman

 A *Song* to Make You Feel Better

"Drifter" by Hippie Sabotage

Notes

_____

_____

_____

_____

_____

_____

_____

_____

_____

_____

_____

_____

_____

_____

_____

_____

_____

_____

_____

_____

_____

_____

Step 2

CREATE BOUNDARIES

Personal boundaries are the lines between your life and personality and those of others. Without them you will become the stronger energies around you, lose all sense of self and live on their terms.
—Lori Harder, *A Tribe Called Bliss: Break Through Superficial Friendships, Create Real Connections, Reach Your Highest Potential*

SETTING BOUNDARIES HAS BECOME a focal point in the narrative around self-love these days, and yet as a millennial generation with our apps and our constant connection to the digital world, we live in a state of perpetual connection. A 2019 Gallup study indicated that not only are we the most stressed we've ever been as a world population, but Americans are among the most stressed people in the world, reporting feeling stress, anger, and worry at the highest levels in over a decade.[6]

---

6   Niraj Chokshi, "Americans Are Among the Most Stressed People in the World, Poll Finds," *New York Times*, April 25, 2019, https://www.nytimes.com/2019/04/25/us/americans-stressful.html.

And again, all this research is largely consistent with what we hear from ManifestHers. They are drained by their work and their relationships; they feel like they are running on empty. They feel like there is a constant stream of responsibility and they are required to be *on* all the time, at work, at home, on social media. They just want to scream "STOP!" and take a few moments back from their day to do something that makes them feel more in control and gives them more agency over their lives.

Sound familiar? Yeah, me too.

YOU KNOW YOU NEED BOUNDARIES

I knew that something had to change. I had been working sixty-hour weeks and felt overworked, overwhelmed, and overextended in every direction. Although I had made the decision to forgive myself for the past and had decided I wasn't quitting, I desperately needed space to think, to breathe, to figure out how to get unstuck and to determine how to help this cause that I had just awoken to: helping women do the same.

If my work had the capacity to get me this bent out of shape right now, I needed to be more deliberate about how much I let it into my life outside of office hours. With my confidence at an all-time low and my overwhelm at an all-time high, I was not acting like myself. It was critical that I create sacred space between the office and me.

I made the decision to turn off my email and messaging notifications on my phone and to schedule into my calendar which times I was in the office and which times I was NOT in the office.

But with my work notifications off and clear boundaries scheduled in to my calendar, I found myself with more than enough space in my life and yet no idea what to do with it.

I started filling it with things that felt fun, things like TV shows and drinks with my friends, going to the movies and finding new restaurants around the city. I couldn't remember the last time I had enough space in my life to just guilt-free enjoy my couch, my relationship, and my dog. Ronnie and I binged the entire *Game Of Thrones* series together.

At first, these things really did feel good. It was as if there had been a store of things that I wanted to get to that had been piling up for a few years that I could finally tap into and enjoy.

But as the weeks passed, I found myself feeling even more anxious than I had felt before when I was overextended and overbooked.

Since my mind wasn't activated by anything meaningful or challenging in the new space I had created, it was constantly wandering. I found myself ruminating again and spiraling out of control. Even though my notifications were off on my phone, I was at the office in my head.

The long nights I spent "numbing out" on the couch with a few glasses of wine watching *GOT* left me feeling depleted and dehydrated. I felt groggy as I went into the office, and I knew in my heart this new lifestyle I thought I needed was not actually enjoyable.

I thought, this space is what I'd needed, so why was I actually worse off now than before?

I realized I didn't want space for the sake of space. I wanted this space to bring new meaning into my life, to give me good energy that I could carry with me in the world, to help me dissect what my inner dialogue meant when she whispered to me at night, "You are meant for more."

I had always been an athlete, and so as my anxiety built and that inner dialogue grew from a whisper to a full-blown scream, I realized that one of the things missing from my life was a physical practice. I needed something that would give me an hour a day to be with, observe, and process all the thoughts running rampant in my mind, and so it was about this time that I found Ritual Hot Yoga, my yoga studio and committed to going to class every weekday at 5:45 a.m.

As I showed up for myself, showed up for the practice and showed up for the mantras, I started putting back together the pieces of me that had shattered in the wake my job change.

I started to build physical strength, and seeing the changes to my body in the mirror gave me more confidence on the mat. I started building strength in my practice, and as I saw my abilities to execute more challenging poses grow, my confidence on the mat grew as well. I started challenging myself more and more. I spent many mornings toppling over, falling on my face, and knocking into my mat neighbors, but the more I tried, the more progress I made. Before long, I was one of the strongest, most advanced yogis in the room.

Every morning as we finished our practice and laid in Shavasana, exhausted from our movement and dripping head to toe in sweat, our instructor would say, "Put your hand over your heart, feel the beat of this essential life-force keeping you alive, and listen to these words: Your life is sacred; this practice is sacred.

Create rituals of pursuing a life that brings you joy. The light and the love in me honors and sees the light and love in each and every one of you. Namaste."

"Namaste."

Each day, I reflected on the mantras on my drive home. What did it mean to treat myself and my life as sacred? What did it mean to create rituals of pursuing a life that brought me joy? What did it mean, *the light and love within me*? Where had the light and love within me gone? I used to feel light, I used to feel love, but I had somewhere along the way lost myself and become unhappy and felt like I had no agency over my life—like I was stuck and had no ability to become unstuck.

As the weeks passed and I continued to grow in my yoga practice, I found my head and heart feeling lighter. Every morning when I woke up with a mess of thoughts and anxieties that had been stewing in my head overnight, I brought them to the mat and grinded through them in my practice. At the end of each practice I would release them into the universe in Shavasana.

BOUNDARIES BRING BLESSINGS

Boundaries make room for blessings.

—Lori Harder, *A Tribe Called Bliss: Break Through Superficial Friendships, Create Real Connections, Reach Your Highest Potential*

Practice by practice, pose by pose, I was creating more space in my mind. My constant stream of thoughts, which had run rampant for years, started becoming observable. I could choose which ones to keep, which ones to listen to, and which ones to grind out in my practice.

The physical movement and the mental exercise of doing this day in and day out allowed me to clear space in my head, and I began seeing clearly again. I started feeling like I had the capacity to take on more things that would bring me joy. This practice had been a blessing, and I wanted to grow even more in this practice of creating space and filling it with joy.

I thought back to when I was a little girl. I used to love reading; I would devour books, completely losing myself in my own head from the comfort of my couch or bed. I had gotten away from reading books during this time, but I knew I finally had the space I needed to start filling my brain with new and exciting stories and ideas again.

CREATING BOUNDARIES IN YOUR LIFE

In a society where we are constantly stimulated and connected, it can be virtually impossible to turn off the world. FOMO is a real thing, and the fear of missing out on a critical work email, a fun opportunity with friends, or anything in between can be scary.

But without creating space in your life, there will be no room for new energy or opportunity to enter.

Ronnie always says, "The definition of insanity is doing the same thing over and over and expecting different results."

Boundaries create space for creation. Saying no to the things you've been doing that haven't been serving you allows you to create space for the new you that's trying to be born.

You picked up this book for a reason. You picked it up and continued reading it because you are feeling stuck, so let me ask you this: If you don't make any changes, how do you expect to have different results?

Your life is sacred. Create rituals of creating boundaries, but be deliberate about what you fill your cup with. Space for the sake of space will do nothing to get you unstuck. Space for the sake of blessings, new ideas, and creation will help you elevate and vibrate at a new frequency, which will ultimately make your head and your heart lighter, priming you for what comes next.

WHAT I DID

I created strict boundaries with no plan for how to use the space that I inevitably found once they'd been created. I felt myself getting even more anxious with these boundaries than I had been before I implemented them.

Once I decided to get intentional about what I was doing to fill that space, I found yoga, which became a safe place where I was able to grow physically, spiritually, and mentally. Yoga helped me restore my confidence at a time when my confidence was at an all-time low and create space in my mind where I had been overextended and overwhelmed.

With this new space, I felt like I finally had the capacity to listen to what my inner dialogue was telling me: "You are meant for more."

My *Challenge* to You

Where in your life do you need to create boundaries to protect your heart and your mind?

When you create those boundaries and that space, how can you be intentional about that extra space to make sure you fill it with things that bring you joy and fill your cup?

What are some of the things you enjoyed doing at a time in your life when you did not feel stuck?

What opportunities do you have to dive into one or a few of these activities with the new space you've created in your life?

 Suggested *Reading*

A Tribe Called Bliss: Break Through Superficial Friendships, Create Real Connections, Reach Your Highest Potential by Lori Harder

A *Song* to Get You Pumped for Boundaries

"No Scrubs" by TLC

Notes

_____

_____

_____

_____

_____

_____

_____

_____

_____

_____

_____

_____

_____

_____

_____

_____

_____

_____

_____

Step 3

FIND YOUR VISION EXPANDERS

Who today is living the life you want to live in your future?
—Anonymous

CREATING BOUNDARIES AND FILLING my space with only things that brought me joy reopened another door for me that I forgot existed, a door into the wonderful world of reading. It was something that had brought me so much joy when I was younger but had ceased to be part of my life once I'd started my professional career.

I found myself leaning into books and podcasts and articles about massively successful entrepreneurs and entertainers whose stories I had always been curious about.

I went all out, learning about the lives of entrepreneurs like Jeff Bezos, Elon Musk, Bill and Melinda Gates, Larry Page and Sergey Brin, Emily Weiss, Alli Webb, Sally Helgesen, Lori Harder, Gabby Bernstein, Cara Alwill Leyba, Barbara Baekgaard, Elizabeth

Cutler and Julie Rice, and my favorite comics, Kevin Hart, Tiffany Haddish, and Ali Wong, as well as other people I admired like Ruth Bader Ginsburg, Michelle Obama, Malala Yousafzai, Jay-Z, Pitbull, Beyoncé, Oprah, Lady Gaga, Ellen DeGeneres, Emilia Clarke, Khloe Kardashian, Emma Grede, Kylie Jenner, Kris Jenner, Elaine Welteroth, and Lewis Hamilton.

I was fascinated by their stories and fantasized about meeting them all one day and inviting them to my home where we would sit at one big table together and share stories about how each of us had disrupted an industry in our own way.

I loved this fantasy, and every time I read another inspiring entrepreneur's journey, I added them to my guest list. But it was just that—a fantasy.

At one point in one of these books or podcasts, the question was posed: "Who today is living the life you want to live in your future?"

All of the above, I thought—basically, everyone who had a clear vision for what they wanted to create in their life, who went out and created it and then became massively successful. I envied them. I envied them because I didn't know what I wanted. I knew I wanted to be massively successful and I knew I had a lot to offer the world, but bringing definition to a vision for my life beyond that was impossible.

I was reflecting on this question with a friend who pointed me in the direction of Lacy Phillips, a manifestation advisor and expert. She often talks about expanders as people who have a similar life experience as you, and who have achieved the same success you're after, and how to leverage them as both inspiration and evidence that whatever it is you want to accomplish is possible because they've proved that it can be done.

According to research, young adults who were at risk for falling off track but had a mentor are 130 percent more likely to hold leadership positions.[7] Expanders are like mentors but more accessible, because as long as you have an internet connection, you can access their content, stories, and infinite wisdom on your own time, go as deep as you need to go, and always come back to them when you need them. And while a formal mentoring relationship may be hard to come by, the positive impact they have on young adults is undeniable, which makes finding expanders a wonderful and entirely accessible alternative.

MY FIRST VISION EXPANDER
Alex Banayan, like me, woke up one day (he was eighteen instead of twenty-seven) feeling stuck. He was a pre-med student at USC and couldn't convince himself to study a day longer. He was on his prescribed path and it was killing him. He had no idea what he wanted to do, but he knew he did not want to pursue medical school for one more day.

Instead of studying, he found himself devouring books on entrepreneurship and the world's most incredible business people and creatives—Bill Gates, Warren Buffet, Steven Spielberg, and countless others. To his disappointment, these books only talked about these people as middle-aged, successful entrepreneurs;

---

7 "Mentoring Impact," MENTOR: The National Mentoring Partnership, accessed December 27, 2019, https://www.mentoring.org/why-mentoring/mentoring-impact/.

they totally neglected their come-up stories. What did they do when they were eighteen that set them apart from the rest?

A fire burned in Alex; he had to know. He wanted to seek them out and ask them in person so he could learn from them, document his findings, and share those with his buddies and ultimately the rest of the world so they could know too.

It took him more than seven years, but Alex did everything he set out to accomplish: he met with all the people he most admired and documented the secrets of their come-up stories for the world to enjoy.

Alex Banayan's *The Third Door: The Wild Quest to Uncover How the World's Most Successful People Launched Their Careers* is accurately described as "the larger-than-life journey of an eighteen-year-old college freshman who set out from his dorm room to track down Bill Gates, Lady Gaga, and dozens more of the world's most successful people to uncover how they broke through and launched their careers."

When Alex started his journey, he was eighteen years old and he didn't come from a VIP upbringing or family. He didn't have any of the connections he needed to get these interviews. This meant that to get in front of the people he most admired, he had to get creative, hiding in a bathroom to meet Tim Ferriss, stalking Steven Spielberg at a party, and chasing Larry King through a grocery store and throwing himself in front of his car. Some of these stories are literally absurd, but you know what? He did it.

He met every single one of the world's most successful people that he set out to meet, and now his journey and his findings are documented for the world to enjoy in his best-selling work, *The Third Door.*

Since publishing, Alex has been named to Forbes 30 Under 30 List and the Business Insider Most Powerful People Under 30 and has been featured in major media including *Fortune, Forbes,* and *Businessweek,* not to mention having presented *The Third Door* framework at business conferences and corporate leadership summits around the world, including at Nike, Apple, and Harvard.

It took me all of a week to read his story cover to cover, I slammed it shut and threw myself back on the couch with my hands in the air. "Holy. Fucking. Shit," I said out loud.

The book is incredible on many accounts, but for me, it was mostly incredible because it was proof that if an average-Joe eighteen-year-old kid with a will and a way could do something extraordinary and in turn create an extraordinary life and extraordinary success out of thin air, then I could do it too.

His book was proof for me that the fantasy I had in my head of one day inviting the most successful people in the world who I admired most over to my house to sit at my table was in fact a possibility.

CHOOSING EXPANDERS WITH INTENTION

Alex was my first vision expander and my complete validation that any vision I had for the future was actually possible.

He expanded my belief that I was not old enough to have massive success. He expanded my belief that in order to reach out to some of the people I most admired, I would have to have something to offer them (instead of just graciously thanking them for all they had offered me through their incredible work). He expanded my belief that I had to have a certain number of accomplishments already under my belt in order to share my ideas or experiences to help others.

After meeting Alex, I started looking back at the people whose stories really stood out to me from all the reading I'd been doing, and I started to realize these people had been expanding me all along.

If Alex Banayan was my validation that anything was possible, Kevin Hart and Phil Knight were my validation that it might take time, but with hard work, dedication, and the relentless pursuit of perfection, you can climb to the top of any industry. It took Kevin more than sixteen years, seven of which he spent on the road perfecting his craft, but Kevin Hart is undeniably one of the most successful comics in history and it took Phil Knight literally decades to build Nike, but to this day he remains undeniably one of the world's most successful entrepreneurs.

If Kevin Hart and Phil Knight were my validation that over a sixteen-year horizon anything is possible, Jeff Bezos was my validation that any person from any background with a vision for helping people and putting the customer's needs first has the capacity to be massively successful, both financially and in terms of massive influence on a world scale. Furthermore, Emily Weiss and Kylie Jenner were validation that regardless of your age or your product assortment, when you build products customers love and you curate the right community to back your brand and your ideas, billionaire status is actually quite achievable, even for women in their twenties.

And if Bezos, Weiss, and Jenner were my validation that there is no cap on the financial success a single individual can have, even at a young age, Tiffany Haddish was my validation that everything in life is truly "figureoutable." Growing up in the foster care system, she was illiterate until high school, she was homeless in her twenties, and she had less than $300 to her name when she decided that stand-up comedy would be her saving grace. Since then, she's managed to become arguably the most famous female stand-up in the world, winning an Emmy and being nominated for a Grammy for Best Spoken Word Album for her performance of the book she wrote, *The Last Black Unicorn*. Yes, she was illiterate until high school, and not only is her book a bestseller but her performance of her reading her own book was nominated for a freaking Grammy. I'm telling you this badass woman is un-freaking-real.

The more I dove back into the stories of these exceptional people, the more I was convinced that anyone, regardless of their circumstances, has the capacity to live an extraordinary life. If you still don't believe me, just do a quick Google search on Malala Yousafzai.

With each story, I felt expansion, I felt doubt move out and belief take its place. All of these people woke up one day with an inner narrative that told them, "You are meant for more," and when they leaned in, they achieved, they had massive impact, and they were the catalysts of change.

The more I reflected on these stories, the bigger my dreams got, as if the lid I used to keep on how big I could dream had finally been ripped off and tossed out the window.

FINDING YOUR VISION EXPANDERS

What is the life you are fantasizing about? Who today has the life that you fantasize about living in your future? I ask these two questions to every ManifestHer who comes through our program.

Answering the first question proves to be tough for most women. My hunch is this is because it's easy to picture this life in your head, it's easy to feel the sensations created inside of your being when you drift off into fantasy land, but it's harder to describe those sensations aloud.

Answering the second question is a bit more tangible. You can point to the person or people and the things they have, the characteristics you love about them and the life you believe they have, and you can say, "I want that."

Maybe it's a famous actress, or a badass CEO, or your boss, or a great mom you know from down the street. Maybe it's all of the above. It's your fantasy—you decide.

For me, it's a combination of all the badass people I mentioned in the previous section and more. Together, they represent the total person that I want to manifest: I want to be a badass wife, mom, friend, and CEO who is regarded by others as funny, kind, motivational, and influential, with a platform that allows her to change the world in a positive way that empowers women to manifest their biggest dreams. But that's me.

You have to be able to answer this for yourself, and trust me, there's no wrong way to answer this question. This is the life you want to manifest. Here's what some of our ManifestHers have said: "my mom and older sister," "Rachel Hollis and Tony

Robbins," "Beyoncé and Ashley Graham," and "Meghan Markle and Kate Middleton."

My only advice here is the more specific you can be, the better. One of our most wonderful ManifestHers said, "Sophia Loren has always been my biggest icon. She has an absolutely fabulous career where she got to play an array of different characters. She won an Oscar, had a happy, long-lasting marriage, and lived a clean lifestyle that never got her into trouble (well, she did get in trouble for tax evasion once, but we won't talk about that). She lived a quiet, low-key life in her golden years and is still relevant now. I would love to have an acting career like her."

When you don't know where to start, starting with expanders empowers you to envision your life at some place in the distant future where you are essentially embodying whoever it is that is living the life you dream about having in your future. So when we ask the follow-up question "Where do you see your life in ten years?" (which we will ask you in the chapter on goal setting), you have the ability to clearly visualize yourself with the things you admire about that person and their life, but you can adapt it to your own future.

WHAT I DID

I stumbled my way into finding expanders who were evidence for me that anything I wanted to accomplish in life was possible if I was willing to set a vision, take action, and put in the time and effort it would take (multiple decades) to have the type of impact I was looking to make.

Once I'd curated my table of expanders, I was able to lean into the idea that the fantasies I had in my head about the type of impact I could have and the type of success I could accomplish was in fact possible.

This newfound knowledge empowered me to dream bigger and get more clear on what success was for me and what I was dreaming of.

My *Challenge* to You

What person or combination of people have the life right now that you want in your future?

What specifically inspires you about the come-up stories for these people and acts as evidence that the success you desire is possible?

Who specifically expands your belief that over a long enough time horizon, anything is possible?

Who specifically expands your belief that money is a resource that is in abundance and will flow to you when you use your unique skills to create meaningful things?

Who specifically expands your belief that in order to be successful, you have to be an expert at something?

Suggested *Reading*

The Third Door: The Wild Quest to Uncover How the World's Most Successful People Launched Their Careers by Alex Banayan
And the books, documentaries, or podcasts of anyone who is an expander for you!

A *Song* to Get You Primed for Expansion

"Lose Control" by Missy Elliott featuring Ciara and Fat Man Scoop

Notes

Step 4

BREAK THE PATTERN

Your habits are not you. They are you on autopilot.
— Sally Helgesen, *How Women Rise: Break the 12 Habits Holding You Back from Your Next Raise, Promotion, or Job*

"THE AVERAGE PERSON HAS 21,500 DAYS between the day they graduate college and the day they die," said Miki Agrawal to me over the bluetooth speaker in my rental car. I was in San Jose, California, all alone on the road, again, working for a company I loved but doing a job that I just wasn't passionate about. Despite all the self-work I was doing on the side to try and find peace and joy, this job was still eating me up inside.

I had just wrapped up my last business meeting of the day and was debating where I would go for dinner that evening. My hotel was north in San Francisco, where I could easily go and have a lonely hotel room dinner while putting in a few more hours of work before shutting down for the evening, but my heart was telling me to head south to the

Bixby Bridge, in Big Sur, a destination I had been dreaming of traveling to for years.

The fuck? I thought. *That's it? That's all we get?* I did some quick math, and I had somewhere close to 19,675 days left.

Everything in my world came to a screeching halt. *Time had never felt so precious.*

The little voice inside of me that had told me months ago, "You are made for more," perked up again and whispered, "Act now or you will never realize your potential or fulfill your purpose. Time is running out."

I looked at the clock. It was the end of the workday, and I didn't have any night meetings or major projects that were due to be delivered. I had a rental car, and I had been dying to see the Bixby Bridge in Big Sur for years. I felt a magnetic pull on my soul, calling me to go there. As if there were a present waiting for me there from the universe. Call it women's intuition, call it universal intelligence, call it God, call it whatever you want—I swear, the pull was magnetic and I chose to lean in.

I pulled my sunglasses down over my eyes, I turned on my favorite playlist, and I sped off in the direction of the sunset in Big Sur, arriving at the bridge just in time for sunset, and it was magnificent. The sky was on fire with blues and oranges and purples and reds, and the waves crashed against the shore, providing the perfect ambiance for a reflection on all of the experiences I'd had over the last few months diving headfirst into yoga, getting more involved in diversity and inclusion conversations in Chicago, and working on expanding my mind and my beliefs through reading and learning about the people I admire most in the world.

As I drank in the last sips of sunlight, I made a promise to myself that if I had only 19,675 days until I died, I would stop making excuses, take control of my life, and to start making the most out of every single day. I refused to live a life of unmet potential. I refused to stay stuck at the trailhead of my own potential. I refused to waste any more time on earth not walking the path toward the future I was dreaming of. I was ready to take control of my life. I was ready to create. I was ready to become the woman I was born to be. I was ready to ManifestHer.

That evening, as I drove back to San Francisco, it was as if the universe dropped the vision for Manifest into my lap. I had this unrelenting dream to bring communities of women together to support each other and hold each other accountable to realizing their potential and manifesting their dreams. There had to be other women like me out there—women who had a textbook "good life" and yet felt stuck and needed someone to pull them out of their funk, help them become unstuck, and hold them accountable to going after their dreams.

What if I could help them and they could help me and we could all help each other? What if I could create a network of like-minded women who had one shared goal—to help one another on the path toward realizing our potential?

I read once in Elizabeth Gilbert's book *Big Magic: Creative Living Beyond Fear* that if you let an idea linger for too long without taking action, it will find someone else to bring it to life. I'd had ideas before that left me for a different sponsor, so when I felt this idea turning into a fire burning inside me, I knew I had no choice but to take action.

I called my best friend, Tasha. "I have this idea," I said. "I want to try it and I want you to help. Are you in?" I asked.

"What's the idea?" she asked.

"We are going to host a staytreat for ten women, all strangers, all based in Chicago. We are going to bring them together for an entire day. We will combine the conversational tools from Lori Harder's *A Tribe Called Bliss* with tools from Gary John Bishop's *Unf*ck Yourself*, Lululemon's goal-setting program, Amber Rae's *Choose Wonder over Worry*, and some of our own original ideas. We'll facilitate meaningful connection and help the women not only unearth their ambitions but fortify their sense of self, get clear on their future, and feel supported by other ambitious women in a wholesome way so they can take action on their biggest dreams and realize their potential."

"I mean, that sounds phenomenal, but how are we going to convince these women that we are in a position to help them?" Tasha asked.

"Two ways," I said. "First, we are going to position it as peer-to-peer; these are the tools that have worked for us and we are just sharing them. Second, it is 2019, after all—we can pack the day with some luxurious activities, we can have a chef make breakfast, we can bring in a yoga instructor to do some yoga together, we can have a professional hair and makeup team do glam, and then do an empowered photo shoot. We'll end the day with a chef making us dinner. So even if they think the content is a total bust, the women will absolutely have a wonderful day."

"This sounds like a dream come true!" she said.

"With all the serving ware and decor Ronnie and I got for wedding gifts, we honestly have a lot of what we need already on hand to host the entire event. I've run the numbers and in addition to buying a few things and hiring for the various services, as long as we come in on budget, we could basically cover all of our costs. Financially, I will support this, but what I need from you is to help me execute the best staytreat Chicago has ever seen. So what do you say—are you in?"

"I'm in!" she said emphatically.

With Tasha on board, I booked the event space, I booked the team of vendors, and I started making calls to get our first group together.

As the seats started selling out and our first group started coming together, I felt the momentum of this idea; the women around me were craving this kind of connection. I felt rushes of excitement every time a woman agreed to join the event.

Event day came and we executed flawlessly. There were tears, there were hugs, there was love flowing out of every woman. We went nonstop from when the women arrived at 9:00 a.m. to when the women left at 9:00 p.m., and we were utterly exhausted. It was everything we had in us to send a post-event survey out that night, and the next day we awoke to some of the best, most soul-stirring messages we could have ever imagined:

"Manifest changed the way I view creating relationships with women. Put a group of kickass, intelligent, like-minded women in a room and things get real! Human connection and conversation is so powerful and Manifest brought me plummeting back down to earth—I am grounded, my cup is full and I am filled to the brim with so much grace I feel like I could explode!!! Stripped of emotional boundaries. Relieved of hesitation and doubt. Confessed the scariest of fears and biggest of dreams. Revealed scars—ones that we could see and others we can only talk about. Reassured one another that we are not alone on this journey called life. Expressed how our hearts sing, which was followed by a standing ovation of our courage," said one.

"Manifest pushed me to open up and really dig deep. It was really emotional sharing so openly with everyone, but hearing each woman's personal story also helped me to realize I am not the only person dealing with some of these life challenges. The Manifest team really set the tone and pushed us all to dive deep. I cried, I laughed, I cheered, and I walked away feeling full of joy," said another.

And this list goes on and on. The impact we had on the women who sat at our table blew me away. The confidence we gained by creating, curating, and executing such a powerful event blew me away. I had so much doubt going into the event and coming out of it so much confidence that we'd created something that women actually needed, craved, and were missing.

I called Tasha the next week. "I want to do it again," I said. "Are you in?"

BREAK THE PATTERN

At this point, you've forgiven yourself for feeling stuck, you've created boundaries and space in your life for new, more positive energy and momentum to flow in, and you've expanded your vision for life by learning more about the people who you most admire. Something's gotta give, so let me ask you this: What can you do today that will break the pattern?

WHAT I DID

For me, what finally broke the pattern was hearing the finite number of days I had left to live. Hearing that caused me to choose going to the Bixby Bridge, which in turn inspired me to give this idea for Manifest a try. When I called Tasha about it, it didn't have a name. It was just an idea for a staytreat for a bunch of women who I thought might also be struggling with some of the same stuff I was struggling with.

And Manifest was truly just an idea. It wasn't a business and there was no expectation or desired outcome; it was just that an idea that was worth giving a try. As long as I wasn't going to go into debt trying it out and as long as I had a friend who was willing to help, I wanted to give it a try.

But believing in myself, trusting myself that I could do it, broke the pattern in a new way. It forced me out of my stuckness into motion, it forced me outside my comfort zone, it forced me to take an idea out of my head and bring it to life with a team of people, and because it was my personal relationships and my personal brand on the line, it forced me to deliver a staytreat that exceeded even my own expectations. That forward momentum, those positive reviews from the women who had come to our event, called for more of the same.

My *Challenge* to You

What is going to be your break-the-pattern moment?

Using the Miki Agrawal quote, calculate how many days you have left.

Do *something different* when you get to that number. Whatever you would normally do, don't do that. Do something different, maybe something you've always wanted to try or see or do.

Still not sure what to do? One of the questions we ask all of our ManifestHers is, "Do you have any secret passions you would like to pursue? What are they and why?" Now go and do one (or more) of the things on that list.

 Suggested *Reading*

Disrupt-Her: A Manifesto for the Modern Woman by Miki Agrawal

 A *Song* to Make You Hit Your Breaking Point

"Try Everything" by Shakira

Notes

Step 5

FIND YOUR EXCUSE EXPANDERS

Some people want it to happen, some wish it would happen,
others make it happen.
—Michael Jordan

HOPEFULLY YOU HEEDED MY ADVICE and did something after reading the last chapter that broke the pattern.

When we ask our ManifestHers what their break-the-pattern moment will be, they tell us it will be the pursuit of something on their secret passion list. Often, that takes the form of "I want to start a personal blog," "I want to write a book," "I want to start selling my art," "I want to be an event planner," "I want to be a motivational speaker," "I want to perform," "I want to start this business," and much more.

And then they go out and they break the pattern.

The next day, they go home and they come up with a great Instagram handle for their new personal blog page, they sign up for a domain and build a website for their blog, they write a blog post, they publish a blog post, they post about the blog post on Instagram, and it feels so good.

Then, Monday comes, the week stresses them out, the following weekend they have plans so they can't do any work on the blog, the week following that is even more stressful than the prior week and so by the next weekend all they want to do is sleep in, clean their house, and veg out on the couch for a few hours to recuperate.

"That was fun," they say as they think back on the rush of energy they got when they wrote their blog and posted that one post on Instagram, "but I don't have enough time, money, or know-how to actually keep that up." So rather than doing a second blog post, they choose to give up, the site collects cobwebs, they decide to cancel the website renewal.

BREAKING THE PATTERN ONCE WON'T SUSTAIN YOU FOR THE LONG HAUL

Doing this *one thing that one time* certainly disrupted the usual flow of life. It got you unstuck and off the hamster wheel for a hot minute, and even though the unstuckness didn't last, it felt so good that it kind of got it out of your system.

But then the challenge still remains, because as time goes on, the further away from that break-the-pattern moment you get, the more you start to feel that same anxiety, that same stuckness, that same voice coming back and saying to you, "You are made for more."

It's in these moments that you need to come up with a more sustainable plan for not just getting unstuck but staying unstuck and moving with purpose toward a longer-term goal and vision. And that starts with addressing every ManifestHer's three saboteurs: "I don't have enough time," "I don't have enough money," and "I don't have the know-how."

THE THREE SABOTEURS: TIME, MONEY, AND KNOW-HOW
Even after the first Manifest event, I felt the saboteurs trying to resist any more forward progress.

Sure, we'd managed to pull off a single event, but that didn't mean we had it in us to pull off a second one. It took a lot of time and effort to plan; we were lucky we got most of the planning done over the holidays, but how would we possibly plan a second one alongside our full-time work schedules?

Sure, we'd managed to, for the most part, cover the costs of the first event with the prices of the tickets, but I'd depleted my network of people I thought would be interested in coming to the event.

And yes, we received incredible feedback from the women who came to the program, but we'd also managed to surprise and delight them by getting a best-selling author to donate signed books for us to read as a group throughout the day. There's no way we'd be able to get the author to do a second round of donations!

The dream of doing a second event felt too big and too unrealistic, and to think that I could start something that would become a company while working full-time was inconceivable.

IS IT WORKING?
Every ManifestHer who comes through our program is using one, two, or all of these excuses (time, money, and know-how) to

validate why she is unable to manifest the sustained change that she wants for her life. But you need to ask yourself, is it working?

It's not working, and that's why you are here in the first place—because you don't want to believe it anymore. That's what's keeping you stuck and keeping you on the hamster wheel of life you so desperately want off of.

Or do you? Do you actually want this change? Do you actually want to pursue something different in your life?

You will naturally succeed at finding evidence to support the narrative you want to believe about your life.

If you believe something is too hard and that you will fail if you try, you will look around and find a mountain of evidence that supports this narrative as fact. You'll go out of your way to find all the people who failed before you and say, "Look! They failed! If I try, then I will fail, too, so I'm going to sit this one out."

This is what most people do, and honestly this is what you have been doing too. You've been looking around at the supposedly insurmountable challenges ahead of you in pursuing your passions and manifesting your dreams and you've found all the evidence in the world to support the fact that what you want is *not possible*. Doing this keeps you stuck, but it keeps you comfortably stuck because you feel validated that whatever it was you were planning is not achievable anyway, so it's okay that you stay stuck.

But the other side of the coin is true too.

Again, you will naturally succeed at finding evidence to support the narrative that you want to believe about your life.

If you believe something is achievable and that you will succeed if you try, you can also look around and find a mountain of evidence that supports this narrative as fact.

Just think back to what you learned when you started looking at the lives of your vision expanders. Just like you can go and point to all the people who failed, there are absolutely people you can go and point to that started off in a worse spot than you and who achieved even more success than you are actually seeking.

So at this point, the question really becomes: *Do you actually want this change? Do you actually want to pursue something different in your life?*

FINDING EXCUSE EXPANDERS TO HANDLE THE SABOTEURS

After a lifetime of self-sabotage, I was fed up with myself. I was literally fighting a losing battle against myself, and it wasn't serving me.

I was standing still in life and watching people around me succeed in their careers, start companies, write books, build wealth, build families, and I started thinking, *If they can do it, why not me?*

DEFEATING TIME WITH MY TIME EXPANDER

I don't have enough time, I told myself over and over before I started Manifest. "I am too busy," I said. I was working an important job, and it is taking everything out of me to perform well.

Or so I thought, until my dear friend and peer had a baby and I watched as she took on the responsibility of motherhood alongside the exact same job as me and somehow all the hours that used to be so full and so busy now were used to take care of a newborn with no impact whatsoever on her performance at the office.

Well, shit, I thought. If my friend who has the exact same job as me can excel at work and be an incredible mother to her daughter, how can I possibly let time continue to hold me back?

But how could I find the time?

BUILDING A TIME BUDGET

Witnessing my friend take on motherhood expanded my belief that time was something that needed to hold me back. I started thinking about time differently; if I could understand where all my time was going, I could go about *finding* the time in my day to do more with my life.

Fortunately, time can be measured in a quantitative way, so I set out to find where all my time was going.

There are 365 days in a year and 24 hours in a day, which means there are 8,736 hours in a year and 168 hours in a week.

I sat down with a pen and paper and did some rough calculations, pulling out how much time I could definitely account for each week given my current lifestyle. In an average week, I probably spend:

- 56 hours sleeping (8 hrs x 7 days)
- 50 hours at work (10 hrs x 5 days)
- 7 hours getting ready & commuting to/from work (1.5 hrs x 5 days)

- 10.5 hours exercising, including my commute time (1.75 hrs x 6 days)
- 7 hours on social media (1 hr x 7 days)
- 7 hours on entertainment (1 hr x 7 days)
- 15 hours on chores, errands, and other "inconveniences" and life things (~2 hrs x 7 days)

Adding all of this up, I could see that I was spending 152.5 hours per week on things I could most certainly account for, and this is when I was "living my best life" which included putting in fifty hours at work, working out, doing my hair for work, spending time with family and friends, giving Cooper belly rubs, using social media, and watching TV.

Where were the other fifteen and a half hours going? And how much time was that per year? I asked myself.

15.5 hrs/wk x 52 wks/yr = 806 hrs/yr

Wait, what? I have 806 hours of my life each year that are currently unaccounted for? I thought.

806 hrs / 40 hrs = 20.15 workweeks

To put this in perspective, these eight hundred and six hours I had were the equivalent of *more than twenty workweeks*, all of which were currently unaccounted for.

Well, I thought, I've certainly *found* the time I needed to plan our next Manifest event—and even more—without compromising my performance at the office or the life I was already living outside the office!

Take a minute here to create your own time calculator using the same structure as I used above.

ACTIVITY	HOURS/DAY	HOURS/WEEK
E.g. Sleep	8 (x 7)	56
Sleep	x	
Work	x	
Getting ready	x	
Commuting	x	
Exercise	x	
Hobbies	x	
Errands/Chores	x	
...	x	
...	x	
TOTAL HOURS PER WEEK		168
TOTAL HOURS SPENT		(sum of spent)
LEFTOVER		(total-spent)

NOW ASK YOURSELF, *WHAT DO YOU WANT EVEN MORE?*

Now that you see where all your time is going each week, I want you to think of all of those hours you spend as items that you pack into a suitcase for your life every week. This is your life-suitcase, and each week, you get to go on the trip of a lifetime.

After that exercise, you might be blown away by the amount of time you can't account for in your life. I know I was! After all, you have the same 168 hours I have, the same 168 hours your time expander has, the same 168 hours your vision expanders have.

Think of all of that unaccounted for time as a bunch of shit you don't need packed into your life-suitcase that you have to drag around with you for the next week.

Now, let's say you were going on the trip of a lifetime to some-place exotic that you've always wanted to travel to your entire life. If I told you that you can fill up your suitcase most of the way with things you wanted to use and wear during your trip and then any space leftover I was going to fill with rocks, you would absolutely fill that sucker to the brim with the things that brought you joy and you couldn't wait to bring with you on your trip.

So how come you treat your life-suitcase any different? How come you are okay with filling your life-suitcase to the brim mainly with things you are obligated to do (sleep, work, commute) and then the rest of it with rocks?

In her book *Choose Wonder over Worry: Move Beyond Fear and Doubt to Unlock Your Full Potential*, self-help author Amber Rae talks about packing your life-suitcase the same way you pack when you go on a trip, and this visual really resonated with me.

Whenever I am packing for a trip, I generally go totally over-board and pack all of my favorite things that I absolutely can't wait to wear and use when I get to my destination, but when I try to close my suitcase, it just won't zip!

As I evaluate the items in my suitcase as part of my repack effort, the question I have to ask myself isn't "What are the things I don't want to bring with me?" because I want to bring everything! The question is "What do I want to bring with me *even more*?"

I had the honor of meeting Amber Rae during her book tour, and she described a profound moment in her life when a woman asked her to write a list of all of the things she wanted to do in her life. Then, the woman asked her to write another list of all the things that she wanted to do *even more*.

"Everyone thinks life is about saying no to the things you don't want to do, in order to do the things that you *do* want to do, but life is actually about saying no to the things that you do want to do in order to say yes to the things that you want to do *even more*," said the woman.

I know a ManifestMama who has a cute little two-year-old, and who between work, domestic responsibilities, and trying to keep up with her husband, family, and friends, was really struggling to make it to the gym.

When I asked her, "What do you want?" she said she wanted to be a good mom, daughter, wife, worker, and friend. When I asked her, "What do you want even more?" she said, "My self-confidence back."

Needless to say, once we knew what she wanted *even more*, we found a few hours in her calendar that was being occupied by optional social activities, and we cut those out to make room for her to get in evening workouts.

You can do this, too, but you have to get curious about where you are spending your time today:

If you have extra time lying around, you have the opportunity to decide what you want to do with it, whether you want to pack more into your life-suitcase or leave the extra space for new opportunities.

If you have more packed into your life-suitcase than is actually possible, you have the opportunity to get and become more critical about what you want to do *even more* than continue to spend your time this way.

It may not be easy, but trust me, when you start seeing the results and start manifesting what you want *even more*, it will be worth it.

DEFEATING MONEY WITH MY MONEY EXPANDER

"I don't have enough money," I told myself. "Any business idea I could come up with would require too much up-front capital for me to start, and I don't know anyone who would be willing to invest, nor would I want to take their money because I am afraid I would not be able to pay it back."

Then, on a bus on my way to the Albuquerque Balloon Festival, I met two successful entrepreneurs who less than twenty years ago had over $700,000 of personal debt and were on the verge of declaring bankruptcy when they decided to swing for the fences and build what is now a multimillion dollar, multilevel marketing company that distributes wickless candles and scented fragrance wax through a network of independent distributors.

During a time of complete financial uncertainty, these two met the original founders at a nearby market and were infatuated with their product. They had no money, but they had know-how, willpower, and manpower, and they told the original founders that they wanted to go into business with them.

Having nothing to lose, the original founders agreed to the partnership and over time, the couple turned the business into a brand that is globally recognized and pulls in hundreds of millions of dollars every year through a consultant network.

It took time, but years later, the couple I met on the bus had not only pulled themselves out of near bankruptcy but have a combined net worth that reaches well into the tens of millions.

Well, shit, I thought. If this couple can figure out a way to bounce back from a $700,000 deficit and become multimillion-aires, how can I possibly let my relationship with money defeat me from moving forward with building my dream?

GETTING REAL ABOUT YOUR RELATIONSHIP WITH MONEY

I'd love to tell you I have great financial habits and have built a financial budget—like my time budget, which I successfully stuck to in order to save up to build Manifest—but the reality is I never actually felt like I was great with money, a mindset I am currently working on shifting to a more empowered one. While I always do the bare minimum—pay my bills on time and always contribute to my 401(k)—I often find that my money in and money out are not in complete alignment.

When I was in my early twenties, Ronnie bought a beautiful six-bedroom, four-bathroom home near Lake Michigan about sixty miles outside of Chicago. We weren't married or engaged at the time, but I knew that he was the person I wanted to share my life with and so, unprompted by him, I took it upon myself to furnish the interior of the home so we could go about renting it as an Airbnb property, and I did this all on credit.

Ugh, I know! It felt so good at the time seeing all the things filling our new home and creating a beautiful, picture-perfect world that I knew future renters would absolutely fawn over, but as my debt piled up, I started to really struggle in my relationship with money.

In Jen Sincero's book *You Are A Badass At Making Money: Master the Mindset of Wealth*, she mentions that most people have a similar relationship to money as they do to sex. "We're all having it," she says, "but no one is talking about it!" So even though we are all having lots of experiences with money, since it's awkward to talk about, we just don't. And when we aren't talking about it and swapping ideas and best practices with one another, we're really not getting any better at it!

> When it comes to having sex and making money, you're supposed to know what you're doing and be all great at it, but nobody teaches you anything about it.
> **—Jen Sincero,** *You Are a Badass at Making Money: Master the Mindset of Wealth*

The cure? Talk about it!

I'm still in the process of paying down the debt I created and perpetuated in my early twenties, but recently I opened up about it with some ManifestHers and it was as if the shame of my debt was lifted the second the words leapt off my lips and slipped into the ethos.

"No one is perfect, and no matter who you are, we are all on our own journey," they soothed me.

While in the past, my Achilles heel was my relationship with my money. Now that I am speaking about it and actively rewriting the narrative I am telling myself about my relationship to money, I am starting to manifest a better relationship with my financial life.

So here's my advice on money and building a financial budget: Be real with yourself; know what you have going out the door and what you have coming in. Monitor the money you have going out, and if there are services you signed up for but are no longer using, cancel them. Think *a penny saved is a penny earned*, and even small amounts add up over time!

Take time every month to evaluate your financial status and recalibrate based on upcoming expenditures and any unexpected expenditures that set you back the previous month. The more time you spend looking at your money, thinking about your money, and getting real about your relationship with money, the more confident you will be in your ability to build a better relationship with money.

At the same time, don't hold yourself back from being happy or taking forward action because of your relationship with money.

You can have excuses or you can have success; you can't have both.

—Jen Sincero, *You Are a Badass at Making Money: Master the Mindset of Wealth*

When I started dreaming of Manifest, you better believe I had big dreams of a women's wellness center in Chicago in the most modern, elegant space you could possibly imagine, but realistically, I didn't have the financial means to quit my job, rent a space, and then fill it with all of the beautiful things it would need in order to attract customers. I also didn't have the interest to secure financing or the desire to actually leave my full-time job.

So while the excuse of "I don't have enough money" had certainly held me back in the past, when this idea for bringing women together came to me and was unshakable, I found a creative alternative: starting a business that didn't require me to leave my job and that would leverage many of the things I already owned and space I was already paying for to start building toward the bigger dream of the future.

One of the beautiful things about this "one step at a time" building process for us is that it has enabled us to stay flexible with the vision for Manifest and to steer our strategy in the direction of the ever-evolving interests of our community of ManifestHers.

Because we are not tied to a physical location, we get to curate even more unique experiences for our members, which enables us to deliver once-in-a-lifetime opportunities to our community members. This novelty is something our members love about what we provide.

Regardless of what your relationship is with money, know that the same possibilities that existed for us exist for you as well. Whatever it is you are dreaming up, there is absolutely a way.

Now, you may have to get creative on where you start your journey, but if money is the only thing standing between you and your potential, remember: You can have excuses or you can have success; you can't have both.

DEFEATING KNOW-HOW WITH MY KNOW-HOW EXPANDER

I don't have the know-how to start a personal development business or program, I thought. *Who would care about or trust my opinion anyway?*

Then I watched as my dear friend, Lindsay Navama, founder of ThirdCoastKitchen.com and author of *Hungry for Harbor Country*, published her own cookbook focused on Harbor Country, Michigan, and as I walked around Harbor Country one afternoon with my husband going in and out of stores, I saw her book on the shelves selling left and right.

She is not a professional chef; she is not a formally trained cook. She is just a wonderful, smart, culinary-inclined badass who had a vision for bringing something to life that didn't exist before. She set herself on a path to realizing that vision and in less than a year had a beautiful cookbook to show for it with sales to back her up, making her instantly credible.

After seeing my friend succeed in authoring and selling her cookbook, I thought, *How does one become an expert? Who is the governing body on experts anyway?*

I purchased a copy of her cookbook and started making recipes from it, and they were phenomenal, as good or better than recipes from the cookbooks I owned written by my favorite Food Network chefs.

I thought about my friend's publishing journey. What if she had waited for someone to pluck her out of Chicago and give her a permission slip to write this book? It's possible she never would have written it and in turn, the world, myself included, would have never been able to enjoy her creative and delicious meals.

This reflection made me realize that the interpretation of whether or not she was an expert, whether or not her food was any good, was up to me.

I thought about other creative professions where the interpretation of whether or not the creator had worth was up to the consumers of the services, and I realized that is literally *every* profession.

Your customers or the consumers of your goods and services are the ultimate authority on what is good enough for them to buy, use, and continue buying and using.

If you are a comedian, whether or not you are funny is up to the audience. Some people love Kevin Hart and some people hate him.

If you are an artist, whether or not your art has value is up to the consumers of it. Some people may be willing to pay hundreds of thousands of dollars for your art while others may think it's trash.

If you create skincare products, whether or not your products are good is up to the consumers of it. Some women need skincare for oily skin, some for dry skin, and if your products work only for a certain type of skin, it's natural that people with that type of skin use more of your products than others do.

If you build software, whether or not your software is useful is up to the consumers of it. If your software solves problems for a certain type of person in a certain type of company, it's only natural that similar people in similar companies will use your software more than others will . . . and the list goes on and on.

As I reflected on all of this, I realized the story of my friend and her cookbook were strikingly similar to my own story.

I'm no certified life coach, I'm early on in my journey as an entrepreneur, and it's my first time writing a book. At the same time, I have read close to one hundred personal development and entrepreneurship books while simultaneously working for one of the most innovative AI companies in the world that literally wrote the book on how to tell great stories. I'm starting a business that is creating real meaning for women in the world, and all of this knowledge I'm accumulating is real knowledge that makes me an expert of the stage I'm in, doing the things that I'm currently doing.

All creators are judged by the quality of their work, and realistically their work will appeal to some and not appeal to others, but the interpretation of that is up to them. When I started to lean into this idea that the only thing that mattered to me was creating value for the people I could create value for, I felt liberated.

GIVE YOURSELF THE PERMISSION SLIP YOU NEED TO START
There is no authority on know-how or "enoughness" to start. There is no person who is going to pluck you out of your home and give you a permission slip and a slap on the bum and say, "Go now, you are finally enough."

Just like me, just like my friend, and just like the countless creators you most admire, you have the capacity already within you to create whatever you want, but that means you will have to be your own permission slip—you will have to stop waiting for someone to give that to you.

You have to trust that, just like me, just like my friend, and just like the countless creators you most admire, you don't have all the answers—but neither did we when we started, and we still don't, and that's okay!

Trust me, you are enough as you are with all the endless knowledge and potential you already possess. Think of everything you've learned in life so far—you have already learned how to walk, talk, dress yourself, get through school, get a job, manage your time, manage your money, and much much more. This dream of yours is just the next extension of you on your journey.

FEELING FOLLOWS ACTION

One of my best friends and ManifestHers is a top sales contributor and performer for a Fortune 100 software company. She has achieved President's Club status for the last six consecutive years, despite each year the requirements for hitting President's Club getting more and more difficult to achieve.

One day, I asked her, "How do you do it? How do you continue to be the benchmark for success at your company?"

"Whenever I am having a day where I'm not feeling super confident, I force myself to take action by repeating this over and over in my head: *Feeling follows action, feeling follows action, feeling follows action*. Then I take one step forward, and I trust that good feelings will result from that action, and then I take another step forward," she said.

You have everything you need already to defeat time, money and know-how. The fastest way to do it is to recognize that you are never going to be ready and you are never going to feel like you know "enough" to begin, but in order to manifest, you are going to have to move through that uncertainty one way or another. You can choose to do it now or you can choose to wait it out and regret not doing it sooner. Remember: *feeling follows action.*

WHAT I DID

I decided I was fed up with the narrative and the stuckness that was caused by telling myself I did not have enough time, money, or know-how to start pursuing a different life for myself and my family.

I sought out expanders who were the validation I needed to stop making the same old excuses over and over.

I used their stories as the evidence I needed to prove to myself the success I sought was possible.

My *Challenge* to You

Who is your time expander? How does their story
prove to you that you have enough time?
Who is your money expander? How does their story
prove to you that you have enough money?
Who is your know-how expander? How does their
story prove to you that you have enough know-
how?
Are you ready to put your vision and your plan to
pursue that vision on paper?

Suggested *Reading*

When: The Scientific Secrets of Perfect Timing by
Daniel H. Pink
You Are a Badass at Making Money by Jen Sincero
Everything Is Figureoutable by Marie Forleo

A *Song* to Get You Pumped

"Ain't No Mountain High Enough" by Marvin Gaye
and Tammi Terrell

Notes

Step 6

POINT TO YOUR DESTINATION

Are you a wantrepreneur or are you an entrepreneur?
—the internet

I WAS TROLLING THROUGH INSTAGRAM one afternoon long before starting Manifest and landed on a visual that said "Entrepreneur vs Wantrepreneur" and showed a time line of one month. When I first read it, I was offended. As someone who had always been an aspiring entrepreneur, I thought, *How dare they judge me like that? I just don't have enough time or money to start my venture. I will do it eventually—that doesn't make me a wantreprenuer!*

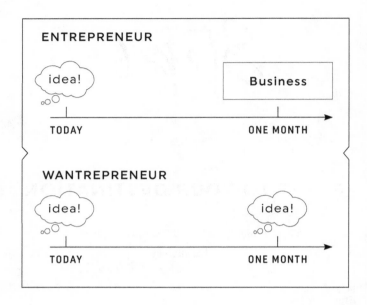

Or does it?

This simple visual has the potential to be terribly offensive in the best way possible because it doesn't simply apply to entrepreneurs. It actually applies to everyone who says, "I want (insert what you want)" and then either does or does not take action to do it.

It draws a pretty clear line between those that *want to* and those that *do*. You are either one or the other, and the options are mutually exclusive and collectively exhaustive. An entrepreneur has an idea, turns that idea into a plan, and in one month has a business. A wantrepreneur, on the other hand, has an idea and it stays an idea in the same one-month time period.

In 1979, Harvard did a study on goal setting and goal achieving that has been widely written about and analyzed because the results of it were so compelling.

Harvard MBAs analyzed the graduating class to determine how many had set goals and had a plan for their attainment. The graduating class was asked a single question about their goals in life: Have you set written goals and created a plan for their attainment?

They determined that 84 percent of the entire class had set no goals at all, 13 percent of the class had set written goals but had no concrete plans, and 3 percent of the class had both written goals and concrete plans.

The results? Ten years later, the 13 percent of the class that had set written goals but had not created plans were making twice as much money as the 84 percent that had set no goals at all. But the 3 percent of the class that had both written goals and a plan were making ten times as much as the rest of the 97 percent of the class.

Say what?

Goal setting and goal getting is real, people! Which is why in this chapter we are going to go headfirst into the exercise of goal setting. Hopefully you are starting to really believe in the idea that whatever it is you want to pursue in your life, you can be successful at it—but just to be certain, I want to introduce you to one more expander.

A GOAL-GETTING EXPANDER FOR YOU

A dear friend and ManifestHer had been saying to me for *years* how she wanted to lose weight and would constantly pick apart her body, which was heavier at the time than she'd ever been before in her life. Two years ago, I started to notice her finally taking action toward that goal; every time I saw her, she looked just a little bit healthier.

Through constant dedication to a fitness regimen, and a balanced diet, she managed to lose over 120 pounds over the course of two years, which completely turned her life around. In celebration of her incredible journey, she went through with a skin removal surgery, tummy tuck, and breast augmentation and is now living her best life. She wears her gorgeous scars out loud for the world to see, evidence of her tireless journey and her incredible feat.

When I asked her why she did it, she said, "I was at my lowest and I felt disgusting. I wanted to be able to find happiness and to sexually express myself with a partner, but I didn't feel comfortable doing that at my size, and so I knew something had to change."

When I asked her how she did it, she said "I knew exactly how much weight I wanted to lose, I knew exactly how good I wanted to feel, I had a clear vision for what I was working toward, and I gave myself exactly two years to achieve that goal."

Some days, she took bigger steps toward that vision than others, but even if they were baby tiny steps, *every single day*, she took steps toward accomplishing that goal.

One of the challenges many of us face in navigating the ambiguity of our post-prescribed lives is we don't get specific enough about what we want or how we are going to achieve it.

We have an idea of it, sure. We have a stitched-together vision of a future that we want, loosely based on our vision expanders who inspire us to want more out of life, but we never take the time to write it out in a way that is as specific as our ManifestHer's two-year weight loss journey:

I lose 120 pounds in two years. I pay two installments in cash for a tummy tuck, breast augmentation and skin removal surgery on (date 1) and (date 2). After my recovery, I wear a size X bikini to the beach to show off my fabulous new body.

And we certainly don't give ourselves space to break those longer-term goals down into more tangible bits:

I lose 60 pounds in one year→which means I lose 30 pounds in six months → which means I lose 10 pounds in 60 days → which means I lose 5 pounds this month → which means I hire a personal trainer this week → which means I research personal trainers in my area today and send three of them (or more) an email inquiring about pricing.

But if we actually did this, if we set aside the time to create an ultra-clear vision for the future we were imagining (regardless of how distant it is) and then backed into that future with specific, measurable, tangible actions, we would find that these big dreams all stitched together in our head are actually quite achievable after all and that by keeping them in our head rather than problem-solving them on paper, we actually make them seem far more complicated than they are.

This is where goal setting comes in.

Goal setting is the ultimate tool for ManifestHers who are ready to step into their purpose by clearly defining their biggest goals and creating a plan to bring to bring them to life.

GOAL SETTING 101

The law of attraction causes us to attract the things that we are thinking about into our lives, it is important to know what we want! Writing a vision authentic to you takes time and practice, so be generous and let go of needing it to be perfect the first time. You'll know that you're heading in the right direction when you are excited and nervous reading it.

—Lululemon Goal Setting Program

The Lululemon program asks you to start goal setting by creating a ten-year vision for your life and specifically breaking it out across your personal life, your professional life, and your health.

Once you are clear on what your ten-year vision is for the three areas of your life, you start getting more specific by turning those visions into goal statements.

You start with goals for each of the three areas that you will accomplish in ten years, and then you back into what you would have to accomplish in five years to set yourself up for success in ten years. Then you determine what you would have to accomplish in one year to set yourself up to achieve your five year goals. At Manifest, we take this further by having you determine what you would have to accomplish in sixty days, in order to set yourself up to achieve your one-year goal and what you would have to accomplish this week in order to achieve the goal you have for sixty days from now. It sounds almost too simple to be true, but—

> By simply focusing on what you want, you will be aware of opportunities around you that help you achieve your goals.
> **—Lululemon Goal Setting Program**

As evidenced by the Harvard MBA study, goal setting combined with plans to achieve your goals works. I used this goal setting and planning program to achieve every single one of my ten-year post-college goals in under five years. I used this goal setting program to write this book. I continue to use this goal setting program for all areas of my life where I have a strong vision and want to manifest it into reality.

Okay, so where to start?

GOAL PREPPING

Start by closing your eyes. Imagine your life as it was ten years ago. Go to a specific memory of that time of your life—it's easiest for me to anchor myself by taking my age, subtracting ten, and then recalling a specific memory from that year. Get really intimate with that memory. Where were you? Who was around you? What were you most excited about in life at that point? What were the things and people who meant the most to you? Try to get as specific as you can in this memory. What do you smell, what do you taste, what do you feel?

Now open your eyes. Can you imagine telling that person, the you from ten years ago, all that you'd accomplish and overcome and do between that memory and where you are right now? It's pretty ridiculous, isn't it? To think that we've grown so much since that memory.

Okay, write down all the things that your PastHer would have never believed if your PresentHer had told her ten years ago that this would be her life now . . .

Example: My PastHer would never have believed that my PresentHer would be working for one of the most innovative AI companies in the world AND starting a company AND writing a book AND married to the man of my dreams.

_____

_____

_____

_____

_____

_____

_____

_____

_____

_____

_____

_____

_____

_____

_____

_____

_____

_____

_____

_____

_____

_____

_____

_____

_____

Take a moment to reflect on the things you wrote down just now. Isn't it crazy how over a ten-year horizon, the constraints of time, money, and knowledge kind of fade away? Ten years is a long time and so much can change! You are a completely different person today than you were back then, with so many experiences that you couldn't have possibly imagined.

Now assume the same will be true for your ManifestHer looking back on your PresentHer ten years from now. In this next exercise, I want you to imagine that it's ten years from today and you are reflecting on this exact moment and all of the things you've accomplished since you read this chapter and completed these exercises.

Where are you as you have this reflection? What is your age? Who is around you? What are you most excited about in life right now? Who are the people and causes that mean the most to you right now? Who are you a point of inspiration and influence for? What do you feel your purpose is? What are the achievements you've had over the last ten years? Get as specific as you can in this vision. What do you smell, what do you taste, what do you feel?

Now open your eyes and brain dump everything that was just in your head onto this piece of paper.

_____

_____

_____

_____

_____

_____

_____

_____

_____

_____

_____

_____

_____

_____

_____

_____

_____

_____

_____

_____

_____

_____

_____

Take a moment to reflect on the things you wrote down just now. Given the exercise we did just before this one, when you look at the things you have written above, how do you feel about them? Do you feel like you constrained your vision for the future in any way as you dreamt of where you will be ten years from now? How big does this vision feel for you? Is it big enough?

Maybe, like me, you really wanted to reach like hell for a big-ass dream and vision that scared the bejesus out of you, but you didn't . . . Why is that? Did your rationalizing brain get in the way and start coming up with those excuses and constraints again? _"I don't have the time/money/knowledge."_

I feel you. It happens to me too.

The practice of setting your vision & goals is just that: a practice. You will find that your vision expands as you practice the art of removing perceived constraints ("I don't have the money/time/knowledge") and get more connected to what you truly want. Your goals will become more courageous and scary-exciting.
—Lululemon Goal Setting Program

Want to try that again? This time, will you take time, money, and knowledge off the table?

Okay, imagine that it's ten years from now and you are reflecting on this exact moment and all of the things you've accomplished since you read this chapter and completed these exercises.

Where are you as you have this reflection? What is your age? Who is around you? What are you most excited about in life right now? Who are the people and causes that mean the most to you right now? Who are you a point of inspiration and influence for? What do you feel your purpose is? What are the achievements you've had over the last ten years? Get as specific as you can in this vision. What do you smell, what do you taste, what do you feel?

Now open your eyes and brain dump everything that was just in your head onto this piece of paper.

_____

_____

_____

_____

_____

_____

_____

_____

_____

_____

_____

_____

_____

_____

_____

_____

Take a moment to reflect on the things you wrote down just now. Take a moment to compare what you wrote just now to what you wrote five or so minutes ago above. What's different? What's the same? What's that telling you?

Remember, your goals will look a little different every time you sit down to do this. This is a practice, but the practice allows you to get clear on what you want. And when you are clear on what you want, you will be more aware of the opportunities around you that move you in that direction.

Okay, now that you have all your creative juices flowing, next, let's do a fun mind-mapping exercise. As I mentioned above, there are three main domains that Lululemon advocates for in your goal setting practice: your personal life, your professional life, and your health.

Think of the circles below as a magnet for all the things you want in your life in ten years. Inside the circle, put all the things you want to attract in your life for each domain. Use the space around the circle to put the things you don't want in your life.

You can literally write anything here. I put jobs, people, experiences, things, anything in the circle that I want to attract into my life, anything that was part of that beautiful vision. Conversely, if there is anything you've removed from your life in that vision (maybe it's poisonous friendships, financial hardship, health problems, etc.) put them the outside the circle representing something that is NOT in your life in ten years.

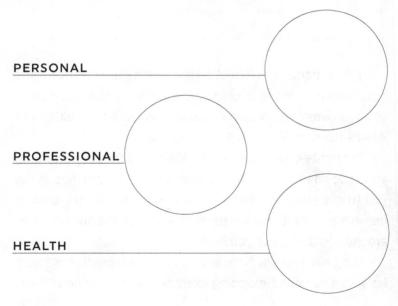

PERSONAL

PROFESSIONAL

HEALTH

GOAL SETTING

Now that you have a really great brainstorm going for what you want for your ManifestHer, what common threads are you seeing? Maybe you want to "buy a home" and "meet my dream partner" or "start my own retail store" or "have children" or "lose weight" or "gain weight" or "make a six-figure salary" or "make a seven-figure salary" or "appear on the cover of Forbes 30 under 30." Whatever your themes are, they should make you *really, really* excited looking at them.

Once you have become more comfortable with the vision you are creating for yourself, it's time to start turning that vision into goals and an action plan. Basically, this means you start backing into that ten-year vision by breaking the vision down into a five-year plan, a one-year plan, a sixty-day plan, and a one-week plan, ensuring you have something tangible and actionable to do by the time you've completed your goal setting exercises.

To start, I always recommend picking the domain of your life that is calling to you most—for me, it's professional, but for some ManifestHers who are single and want to be ManifestMamas one day, they start with their personal domain—and then repeat the exercise for each of the three domains.

Be sure that when you write your goals, the words you use are the outcomes you seek and they are specific, measurable, and time bound. Use phrases like "I am a New York Times best-selling author" as opposed to "I would like to be a New York Times best-selling author."

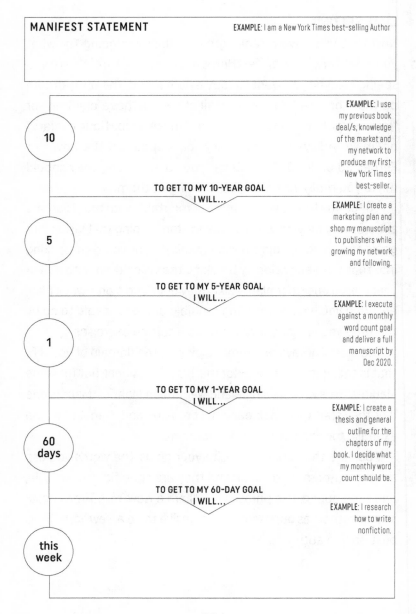

MANIFEST STATEMENT

EXAMPLE: I am a New York Times best-selling Author

10

EXAMPLE: I use my previous book deal/s, knowledge of the market and my network to produce my first New York Times best-seller.

TO GET TO MY 10-YEAR GOAL
I WILL...

5

EXAMPLE: I create a marketing plan and shop my manuscript to publishers while growing my network and following.

TO GET TO MY 5-YEAR GOAL
I WILL...

1

EXAMPLE: I execute against a monthly word count goal and deliver a full manuscript by Dec 2020.

TO GET TO MY 1-YEAR GOAL
I WILL...

60 days

EXAMPLE: I create a thesis and general outline for the chapters of my book. I decide what my monthly word count should be.

TO GET TO MY 60-DAY GOAL
I WILL...

this week

EXAMPLE: I research how to write nonfiction.

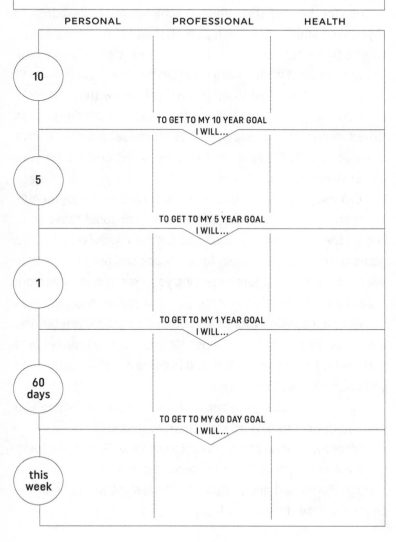

MANIFEST STATEMENT

EXAMPLE: I am a New York Times best -selling author, an amazing wifey/mama, and in the best shape of my life

	PERSONAL	PROFESSIONAL	HEALTH
10			

TO GET TO MY 10 YEAR GOAL
I WILL...

5			

TO GET TO MY 5 YEAR GOAL
I WILL...

1			

TO GET TO MY 1 YEAR GOAL
I WILL...

60 days			

TO GET TO MY 60 DAY GOAL
I WILL...

this week			

GOAL MANIFESTING

Remember, you can do anything. The vision you just put together is yours for the taking, and the plan you put together is yours for the executing. You can achieve your wildest dreams if you stop limiting your own potential and start taking action to get there. It's scary. But it's real. And it's really exciting. Remember what my girl Cara Alwill Leyba says: "Teach yourself to dream without limits, and you will achieve without limits."

Now that you have specific, measurable, achievable, realistic, time-bound goals on paper, look at them. Set a timer for five minutes and meditate on that vision you just created for your life; envision yourself staying the path.

Call your best friend, spouse, mom, college professor, mentor, or anyone else you feel comfortable talking to about these goals and let them know what you just did. Let them know what you are going to try and accomplish for the week and ask them if they will hold you accountable by texting you exactly one week from today to see if you did the thing you said you were going to do.

At first, speaking your goals out loud may be scary, but the more you do it and the more people you tell, the more people you will find both support you and in some cases actually bring you opportunities to help you.

Finally, put your goals somewhere in the open where you can see them and have to face them everyday.

Whenever I finish setting mine, I always say, "Frame and hang, baby! Frame and hang!" I put mine into a cute pink picture frame I bought for myself and put them in plain sight where I can see them and face them everyday.

If you take this advice and frame your goals, when your people come over to hang out at your place, don't take your goals down.

This is the life you are manifesting, so be proud of it! Who knows? Maybe they know someone or something that can help you get one inch closer to that goal.

My *Challenge* to You

Actually do the exercises in this chapter, please. It's for your own good!

 Suggested *Reading*

Your Best Year Ever: A 5-Step Plan for Achieving Your Most Important Goals by Michael Hyatt

 A *Song* to Get You Pumped to Set and Achieve Your Goals

"I'm Coming Out" by Diana Ross
You can't go wrong with this original, but sometimes I listen to "Mo Money Mo Problems" by The Notorious B.I.G. instead. So you get two songs in this chapter ☺. You're welcome

Notes

Step 7

TAKE ONE STEP FORWARD AND THEN DON'T STOP MOVING FORWARD—USE YOUR GOALS TO SET DIRECTION AND USE YOUR HABITS TO ACHIEVE YOUR GOALS

You have the life you're willing to put up with.
—Gary John Bishop, Unfu*k Yourself: Get Out of Your Head and into Your Life

READ THAT AS MANY TIMES AS IT TAKES TO SET IN.

I had seen this book, *Unfu*k Yourself* by Gary John Bishop, on newsstands around the city and in every airport. The title was surprising and the cover art was intriguing. I was on the way back from a trip, bookless, when I finally decided to give it a download on Audible.

I boarded the plane and a Scottish voice played through my AirPods.

Do you hate your job? Are you in a bad relationship? Is there something wrong with your health? Fine, get a new job. End the relationship. Change your diet and exercise or locate the kind of help you need . . . If you're not willing to take the actions to change your situation—in other words, if you're willing to put up with your situation—then whether you like it or not, that is the life you have chosen. Before you think, 'But . . .' or start to get your knickers in a twist . . . let me say one more thing: By defending your circumstances as they are right now, you are actually making a case for being where you are. Give it up.

—Gary John Bishop
*Unfu*k Yourself: Get Out of Your Head and into Your Life*

Life is so different now that you've set those goals, right? Maybe not. Maybe you didn't even do the exercises I provided for you in the last chapter. Maybe you just kept reading because you didn't have a pen, so you just leapfrogged the exercises all together and came straight to the beginning of this chapter.

I'll be the first to admit, I did exactly what you just did before with every self-help book I ever read—that was, until I read *Unfu*k Yourself*.

"I'll come back to these exercises," I told myself, though I never did. And why? I mean, I was reading the book in the first place because I wanted to manifest a change in my life. But I was *so busy* (or so I told myself) that I didn't have enough time or energy to go find a pen and then *do the work*. Then I'd turn the last page on the book, close the cover, put it away, and never pick it up again.

Days, then weeks, then months would go by, and nothing in my life would change. Why? Because I was not willing to do the things I knew I needed to do to manifest change in my life. And honestly, who was this serving? It certainly wasn't serving me! I felt stuck, I lacked confidence, and I continued to live some twisted version of *Groundhog Day*.

> You are not your thoughts, you are what you do.
> **—Gary John Bishop**
> *Unfu*k Yourself: Get Out of Your Head and into Your Life*

The definition of procrastination is the action of delaying or postponing something.

So let me ask you this: *Why would you delay or postpone stepping into the life you were born to live?*

For those of you who feel bad and want to go back and do the exercises now, I'll wait. Because without your goals on paper, you really don't have an anchor or self-accountability for any future action. Remember: You are not your thoughts. You are what you do.

For those of you who still do not want to do the exercises, I want you to remember: Nothing will change if you don't. If you are not willing to change, then you are willing to live with your life as it is. It's okay to not be willing to change—I want to make that clear—but instead of moving forward in this book, consider going back to the start again to remind yourself why you picked it up in the first place.

Finally, for those of you who completed the exercises (and for those of you who actually went back), you have an actionable first step to take this week. Yay! My question for you is: *Are you willing?*

Again, read that as many times as it takes.

Sister, you have the roadmap to your dream life in your hands. You are now in the 3 percent of people who have clear, written goals and a plan to achieve them.

You've proven to yourself that the things you are dreaming about are possible through all the research you did on your vision expanders, as well as your excuse expanders (your time expanders, money expanders, and know-how expanders). At this point, there is nothing more I can do to help you move forward on the path toward your potential; this one is on you.

Are you willing to take the step forward that you need *this week* to set yourself up for achieving your sixty-day, one-year, five-year, and ten-year goals? Or are you willing to continue living life the way it is?

MEET RESISTANCE

If you are like many of our ManifestHers, you are nodding your head to the last question. You are like, "Oh yes, I am *so* willing," but when the time comes to lace up your tennis shoes, to send the email, have a conversation, or to do the research you promised yourself you'd do, you find yourself up against this incredible force that prevents you from doing that one thing you said you would.

I call this tremendous force Resistance, and she is one evil b**ch with the strength and potential to hold you back for as long as you'll let her.

She is your inner hater who, despite all the evidence you've provided, refuses to accept that you are ready to step into the unknown. She argues with you in the form of prevention and inaction.

And honestly, you can't hate her too much. She has successfully protected you your entire life, and she's strong and confident because she's done a good job of it, considering you are still alive to read this!

But she serves a distinct purpose: to keep you safe, to keep you in your comfort zone. If she could have it her way, she would keep you at the trailhead of your potential for your whole life because once you start walking the path, you will quickly get outside your comfort zone, and outside of your comfort zone is the unknown, and the unknown scares the living shit out of Resistance.

But as much as you can empathize with Resistance and her cause, she is the reason you feel stuck in the first place. It's time you let her know that you are going to move forward anyway.

YOU CAN DO ANYTHING HARD FOR TEN SECONDS

In the show *Unbreakable Kimmy Schmidt*, there is a scene where the main character, Kimmy, is reflecting on her time as a sister-wife and says a human can do anything for ten seconds. Anytime Kimmy has to do something that is really hard, she does it, and while she does it, she counts to ten.

When I started down the path to build Manifest and to write this book, Resistance was a main character in my life. There were so many things I didn't want to do, so many things that truly pushed me outside of my comfort zone, but when I was left with the choice to be willing to change or to be willing to stay the same, I knew in my heart of hearts I wanted to change. So I took action, dragging Resistance right along with me.

At one point in my career, I was a product manager, basically a person responsible for creating ideas for new things for people to use. There were lots of ideas that I wasn't sure we could actually bring to life, so I worked with a team of engineers who helped me determine whether an idea was in fact feasible.

There were some sessions where the engineers would tell me, "We are virtually certain that this idea is impossible!"

To which my response was always, "Virtually certain and absolutely certain are two different things." I would tell them, "Time-box it—give yourself a specific amount of time to do the research and then make a decision. Why don't you give yourself one hour to research whether or not this idea is impossible and then let me know."

Often, they would come back to me after an hour and tell me that they'd come up with a way to do it, and then we would go about bringing the "virtually impossible" idea to life together and delight our customers.

I decided to apply this idea that (1) I could do anything hard for ten seconds and this separate but related idea that (2) I could time-box tasks that felt challenging or virtually impossible to my goal-getting plans.

"I can do anything hard for exactly one hour," I told myself and then set a timer for exactly one hour and put my head down and got to work.

Every time I did this, the timer would go off sooner than I thought it would and I would feel a rush of good energy. Then

I would look at my calendar and find another one-hour time block that I could use to continue doing the work and schedule a meeting with myself to do it. When that meeting came, I would set a timer for one hour and put in the work.

YOUR GOALS AREN'T ENOUGH ON THEIR OWN

I'll be the first to tell you that while goals are great, they are not enough on their own to ensure you manifest the change you want in your life. Your goals are simply the vision you've cast for your life, the reality you want to create for yourself, but without action, you can never attain that vision and you can never make that your reality.

While you should be dedicated to your goals and let them act as a compass for your actions, you have to be just as dedicated to the actions as you are to the goals. The process is just as important as the goals themselves.

"Forget about goals. Focus on systems instead," suggests James Clear in *Atomic Habits: An Easy & Proven Way to Build Good Habits & Break Bad Ones*. When I first read this, I was seriously skeptical—forget about my goals? But I kept reading. While goals are good for setting direction, James suggests that there are four problems with goals, and honestly, you really can't deny him on these:

The first problem with goals, he suggests, is that winners and losers have the same goals.

Hmm, I thought. *Well, I guess he is right.* Take a sports example: both teams have the same goal—to win the game—but at the end of the game, one team achieves it and the other does not. *Okay, maybe he is on to something,* I thought.

The second problem with goals, he suggests, is that achieving a goal is only a momentary change. Take, for example, your goal to clean your room. You summon up the energy, you get it clean, and that feels great. But if you are a sloppy person, a day, maybe two, goes by and your room is dirty again. So, you did achieve your goal, but it was only momentary.

Okay, I thought, *another good point.*

The third problem with goals, he suggests, is that goals restrict your happiness. "The implicit assumption behind any goal is 'Once I reach my goal, then I'll be happy,'" but this basically means you give up any enjoyment of the process. And let's be clear: we set goals on a ten-year horizon in the last chapter, so that would mean you are giving up on any joy in the next ten years. And the reality is that your actual path will stray from the journey you had in mind when you set out, so it really makes no sense to restrict your happiness to only the scenario where you follow the path you laid out for the next ten years, achieve your goals, and then choose to be happy.

Well, he's definitely right about that one, I thought.

The fourth problem with goals, he suggests, is that goals are at odds with long-term progress. Think about a runner whose goal is to run a marathon. They train, they run, they cross the finish line, and then boom, goal achieved. "When all of your hard work is focused on a particular goal, what is left to push you forward after you achieve it?" he asks.

In just a moment of reflection, I thought about the stuckness I felt once I had achieved ahead of schedule all my ten-year goals I'd set back in my college years. *Okay*, I thought. *You win, James. I'll meet you in the middle—goals and process are equally important. Without goals, the processes you focus on aren't clear, and without processes to focus on, you don't achieve your goals.*

"You do not rise to the level of your goals. You fall to the level of your systems," he says. "Bad habits repeat themselves again and again and again not because you don't want to change but because you have the wrong system for change . . . What is left out of the goal is the system, the process, the work that enables you to achieve it."

Do I think you should actually forget about your goals and focus entirely on your systems and process? No, I don't. Do I think you should keep your goals at the top of your mind while simultaneously working on your process and habits every single day so you take steps in the direction of your goals and never stop? Well, yes. Yes, I do.

A PROCESS TO HELP YOU BUILD A SYSTEM THAT WORKS

Since you have the roadmap from the last chapter for what you need to do, I want you to do this: Find one hour on your calendar and schedule in that task. When that hour comes, I want you to keep that meeting, because that is a meeting with your future-self—that is a meeting with your ManifestHer.

And when you sit down to do that task, no matter how hard it is, I want you to repeat this over and over in your head or out loud: "I can do anything hard for ten seconds. I can do anything hard for ten seconds," until the hour is up.

Once you've completed this, I want you to find another hour in the next seven days and schedule that on your calendar. Again, when that hour comes, I want you to keep that meeting, because that is a meeting with your future-self—that is a meeting with your ManifestHer.

Repeat this process over and over, increasing the frequency of your meetings with your ManifestHer as you get more comfortable with the process. As you do this, see if you can find joy in the process, because if you are acting in the direction of your dreams, then even when the work is hard, you should feel a spark of joy, some level of exhilaration and accomplishment.

Take notice of the momentum starting to build. Once you complete a task, notice how the next one seems more apparent; notice how the accomplishment of completing the last task actually inspires you to want to do the next one.

Remember: "The secret to getting results that last is to never stop making improvements. It's remarkable what you can build if you just don't stop," says James Clear in *Atomic Habits*.

NEWTONIAN PHYSICS

Let's nerd out for a second: in Newtonian physics there is a concept that postulates that if an object is at rest or in motion, it will remain at rest or in motion unless it is acted upon by an equal and opposite force. Momentum is a function of an object's mass and velocity.

The point here is, once you've taken your vision for life and unstuck it by your sheer will to do something hard for ten seconds, you've done the hardest part—you've got that thing, that idea, in motion. It now has momentum. It is literally a law of physics that once something is in motion unless it is acted upon by an equal and opposite force, it's going to stay in motion. Ideas build mass and velocity when you spend time on them and when you share them with others. So now that you've got this thing moving forward, your new role is to do whatever it takes to clear the way for it, making absolutely certain that the opposing forces trying to act on it are unable to do so.

I called Tasha. "I want to do it again," I said. "Are you willing to do it with me?"

She was.

We scheduled an hour to discuss feedback from our first event. We scheduled another hour to discuss changes to our format for the next event. We scheduled another hour to reach out to the vendors we would need to meet with to host our second event. We scheduled another hour to reach out to some of the people in our network we thought would benefit from our event. The second event came and we executed. We sent surveys to the ManifestHers from our second event and they gave us both fantastic and constructive feedback.

We scheduled an hour to discuss feedback from our second event. We scheduled another hour to discuss changes to our format for the next event. We scheduled another hour to reach out to the vendors we would need to meet with to host our third event. We scheduled another hour to reach out to some of the people in our network we thought would benefit from our event. The third event came and we executed. We sent surveys to the ManifestHers from our third event and they gave us both fantastic and constructive feedback.

We felt momentum carrying us forward from event to event. We started to feel repeatability in our processes and our preparations for the events. We felt momentum from the women around us and as time went on and we continued to build our business one hour and one event at a time, we went from one event to twenty events. We went from $100 in revenue to over $15,000, we went from zero community members to one hundred, and we went from a team of two to a team of four.

Was it easy? No.

Did it bring us joy? Yes.

Why? Because we had finally left the trailhead of our potential and were walking the path.

Yes, there were days I woke up absolutely exhausted. I was a daughter, sister, friend, dog mama, and a brand new wife. I was working a full-time job, writing a book, and starting a company. But when I thought about the alternative, feeling stuck, feeling complacent, feeling like I was made for more but not taking action toward that future, I knew I would choose joyfully exhausted every time.

My *Challenge* to You

Go back and do the exercise in this chapter then take notice of the momentum you build through that process. Journal about it.

Reflect on how to continue focusing on the habits and processes that help you build and maintain momentum.

Notice how your goals might evolve as you take steps forward—that's okay. That's what happens when you start walking the path: the path starts revealing itself. You and the world around you cocreate new goals and evolve your existing ones when you start focusing on the processes that are driving you in the direction of your goals.

 Suggested *Reading*

*Unfu*k Yourself: Get Out of Your Head and into Your Life* by Gary John Bishop

Atomic Habits: An Easy & Proven Way to Build Good Habits & Break Bad Ones by James Clear

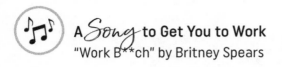

A Song to Get You to Work
"Work B**ch" by Britney Spears

Notes

_____

_____

_____

_____

_____

_____

_____

_____

_____

_____

_____

_____

_____

_____

_____

_____

_____

_____

_____

Step 8

USE FEAR AS YOUR COMPASS

Inside our minds there is a nasty little voice, a saboteur, a censor, and an eternal critic who creates a constant stream of scathing remarks that are usually disguised as The Truth. I call this voice Worry. {But there is also a second voice}, a much more kind, compassionate, and curious one. One that wants us to do well, be seen, and pursue that which we most desire. One that knows with all of its knowing our truest truth. That voice is Wonder.
—Amber Rae, *Choose Wonder over Worry: Move Beyond Fear and Doubt to Unlock Your Full Potential*

ALTHOUGH OUR MANIFEST EVENT BUSINESS was building momentum and we started getting wonderful word-of-mouth referrals from women who had been through our program, every single time I put money down for an event, booking the space, booking the vendors, purchasing all the products we needed to curate an amazing experience for our ManifestHers, I felt fear.

Fear is caused by the feeling that something is dangerous and therefore likely to cause pain.

I feared not being able to deliver a great experience for the women at our table. I feared not being able to cover the cost of the event by not finding enough women who felt the need to be at the table. I feared vendors not showing up and delivering their services so we could provide a wonderful experience for our ManifestHers. I feared our ManifestHers somehow misinterpreting what the event was going to be about, coming, having a miserable time, and then telling their friends that Manifest was one big fraud.

And you know what? Pretty much all of our fears came true. Tasha and I would be freaking out because what we feared most was coming true. We had ManifestHers contact us last minute to drop out and cause us to go into the red on our event profit. We had a key vendor cancel last minute and we had to get scrappy to make sure our ManifestHers would never know the difference. We had our space get double-booked and had to chase out another group that thought they had rented the space.

HOW FEAR BECOMES YOUR COMPASS

Literally every fear we imagined reared its ugly head at one point or another.

I remember specifically in fall 2019, after looking at feedback from our more than one hundred community members, we decided to launch a program called Manifest Mondays, a sixty-minute video call Monday nights that would be free to all members of our community and would act as a check-in for women who needed that weekly accountability partner to change their habits, focus on their systems, and achieve their goals. I was excited about the format and initiative, and I was convinced this thing was absolutely what had been missing from our offerings.

We'd been promoting the event for a few weeks, we had tons of women RSVP to attend, and although I was so excited to bring this new idea to life, I had butterflies in my stomach all day. Would people show up? Would my team deliver? We had just brought on a new team member and she would be attending. What would she think of it all? What would she think if we had poor attendance? Would she regret her decision to join us?

That night, the whole Manifest team, including our new team member, jumped on to participate in the first ever Manifest Monday. Five minutes went by, then ten, then fifteen, and not a single woman from our community, not even the women who had RSVPd, showed up to the call.

After twenty minutes of just the four of us, I told the team that we could all jump off. "No one is coming," I sulked.

We hung up the video call and I was mortified. What an embarrassment! I was so ashamed. My worst-case scenario had come true. Literally not a single person showed up. Where had we gone wrong? I thought this was what the community wanted. How could we have been so off? And, lord! What would our new team member think? She'd just joined our team and this was her first experience doing an event with us? Ugh. I wanted to bury my head in a hole and not come back out until, well, never. I knew the next day I was going to see some of the women from our community and they would ask me how Manifest Monday had gone, and what would I tell them? It didn't? Ugh. This was going to be so embarrassing. "I'm a failure," I concluded.

And then my phone buzzed. A text message from our new team member. It was everything I had in me to look at it. I unlocked my phone and went to her text and in all of her knowingest wisdom, she said, "Knowing what won't work is just as important as knowing what will work. This is one of the greatest gifts we could have asked for. This is a compass pointing us to where we go from here."

I read and reread her wise words until I started to feel better. She was absolutely right.

REDEFINING YOUR RELATIONSHIP WITH FEAR

Fear is the emotion that tries to prevent *failure*, and *shame* is the emotion you feel when *failure* inevitably happens. We perceive these emotions as being negative because they surround a circumstantial outcome that we've been told *is* negative.

But what if failure has been wrongly assigned a negative connotation and we've been misinterpreting it as negative? What if failure was actually growth?

> *When we learn to stop seeing the experiences in our lives as a reflection of our unworthiness and not enoughness, we'll see them for what they truly are: a signal that we had the courage to get in the arena and give it our all.*
> —**Amber Rae,** *Choose Wonder over Worry: Move Beyond Fear and Doubt to Unlock Your Full Potential*

That night, we were in the arena and we gave it our all. We pushed through fear to be there and without having pushed through that fear, we would have never failed. Even though I felt shame from that experience, I was reminded through my interaction with our new team member that:

> If we can share our story with someone who responds with empathy and understanding, shame can't survive.
>
> **—Brené Brown,** *Daring Greatly: How the Courage to Be Vulnerable Transforms the Way We Live, Love, Parent, and Lead*

CHOOSING WONDER OVER WORRY

When you start down the path toward your potential, even though you have momentum, you will absolutely experience fear, you will absolutely experience failure, and you will absolutely experience shame.

But when you self-impose the idea that fear, failure, and shame are bad emotions, you are misinterpreting their purpose.

Fear is what shows you that you are close to growth. You wouldn't fear failure if you had done something before; you fear failure when you are doing *something new*, and when that *something new* is on the path to your potential, it is exactly what you need!

What if you flipped the script on fear and let it be your compass as opposed to your detractor?

As you continue on down the path of realizing your potential and bringing your ten-year vision to life, there is one guarantee I can make: you will absolutely experience fear and failure and shame.

And when these feelings come on, they generally come on strong and fast and together like one big momentum-killing gift set, compounding one another and sending you spiraling out of control and into paralysis mode.

In the last chapter, I talked about Newtonian physics, and I said that an object in motion will remain in motion unless it is acted upon by an equal and opposite force.

Fear and shame are two of the most powerful forces out there trying to prevent your forward momentum, and if you are not careful with them, they can stop you dead in your tracks.

As much as these negative feelings drain you and try to kill your momentum, there is one fortunate thing about them: they are just feelings, and feelings are experienced by you, which means you get to choose how you interpret them and to what extent you allow them to exist alongside your momentous vision, your goals, and your action plan.

WHAT I DID

I started believing that I *should* feel fear but reminding myself that it is circumstantial and it is a compass for me on the path to realizing my potential.

I started believing that I *should* have failures but those failures were circumstantial. I was not a failure, and failing is just as important as succeeding. Knowing what wouldn't work was just as important as knowing what would.

I started telling myself that it was *okay to feel ashamed* but reminded myself that shame is also circumstantial. Having a failure can feel shameful, but that doesn't make me *inextricably* bad or *inextricably* a failure.

I reminded myself that shame is what you feel when you put your heart on the line, and there was nothing shameful about trying with my whole heart to bring Manifest to life so it could help countless women realize their potential.

My *Challenge* for You

How is fear coming up for you right now? What opportunities do you have to flip the script on fear and leverage it as your compass?

How is failure showing up in your life right now as you walk the path to realizing your potential? How can you observe these failures as helpful indications of what won't work and give them just as much meaning as successes, which show you what will work?

How is shame showing up for you right now? What opportunities do you have to share your shame with someone else so you don't have to carry it around or ruminate on it any longer?

 ## Suggested *Reading*

Choose Wonder over Worry: Move Beyond Fear and Doubt to Unlock Your Full Potential by Amber Rae

 ## A *Song* to Help You Tell Fear, Failure, and Shame, "Sorry, Not Sorry"

"Sorry, Not Sorry" by Demi Lovato

Notes

Step 9

TAKE TIME TO REST AND RECALIBRATE

It does not matter how slowly you go as long as you do not stop.
—Confucious

WHEN WE FIRST STARTED MANIFEST, the format of our program was such: ninety minutes of personal introductions around the table, where each of the women would talk about who they were, what they were most proud of and excited about in life, and then what they were most nervous about or scared of. After introductions, our ManifestHers would move to a separate room for a conversation led by Tasha around self-love for an hour before I met with them to do a guided meditation and a facilitated goal-setting workshop.

When I met up with our ManifestHers after their self-love conversation, I would say, "Self-love is something I've struggled with my whole life. In fact, it's one of the reasons I need Tasha as my partner, because she's mastered the art of self-love and I am a beginner on my journey."

In conversations with Tasha leading up to our first Manifest event, we talked a lot about the perception of self-love in the United States and how we took issue with it.

Google or IG search #selflove or #selfcare, and I guarantee you will find pictures of Instagram influencers selling bath bombs and skin care products with some kitschy caption that ends in #ad. And now, don't get us wrong, we love a good bath bomb, we love a good spa day with a massage and a facial, but the narrative around self-love needs to go deeper than that.

DEFINING SELF-LOVE AND SELF-CARE

When we googled "self-love" and "self-care," we started to see the problem:

Self-love: regard for one's own well-being and happiness (chiefly considered as a desirable rather than narcissistic characteristic)

Self-care: the practice of taking action to preserve or improve one's own health

But when we looked at the words *self*, *love*, and *care* separately, the definitions were vastly different:

Self: a person's essential being that distinguishes them from others, especially considered as the object of introspection or reflexive action

Love: an intense feeling of deep affection

Care: the provision of what is necessary for the health, welfare, maintenance, and protection of someone or something

A deep affection ... the provision of what is necessary for the health, welfare, maintenance, and protection ... your own essential being ...

When I started to reflect on the people and things in my life I felt a deep affection for, I thought, my husband, my mom, my dad, my brothers, my grandmothers, my grandfathers, my friends, my dog, my ... then I paused to think. I did not make my own list.

I asked Tasha, "Who do you have a deep affection for?" Tasha didn't make her own list either.

The epidemic was more widespread than just this. We asked all of our ManifestHers, "Who do you have a deep affection for?" Not a single one of our ManifestHers made her own list either!

Our current narrative around self-love and self-care is flawed, we concluded.

REDEFINING SELF-LOVE AND SELF-CARE THE MANIFESTHER WAY

Self-love is not a facial and a bath. Self-care is not going to Soul Cycle and brunch with friends.

Self-love is an intense feeling of deep affection for your essential being. Operating under this new definition becomes more and more important as you walk the path to your potential where you are absolutely going to expose yourself to fear and failure and shame and resistance and a host of new people and a complete spectrum of experiences.

Self-care is the provision of what is necessary for the health, welfare, maintenance, and protection of your essential being.

Operating under this new definition is also critical to your sustained success on the path to your potential.

SELF-LOVE AND SELF-CARE IN PRACTICE

In the summer of 2019, Tasha and I teamed up with a corporate partner to do an eight-week wellness series in downtown Chicago. At the time, she was living two hours south of the city, and so every Sunday, she was driving up to be present for our ManifestHers.

Every week as we drove to the studio, we talked about how anxious we were. Would the content we had planned for that day resonate? How would our ManifestHers feel about the topics and our ability to facilitate meaningful conversations?

At the end of the eight weeks, the feedback surveys came in and the outcome was that the program was incredibly positive and impactful. I couldn't wait to provide a readout to the CEO of the studio partner letting her know that she had made a great choice partnering with us.

And at the same time, I felt conflicted on the tone of my message and suggested next steps.

This partnership was the most money Manifest had made all year. The program was so impactful, it helped one ManifestHer get a promotion, another ManifestHer launch a speaking career, another ManifestHer launch a holistic wellness company and finally start authoring a book she'd been wanting to write, and another woman have a difficult but necessary conversation that led her to finally putting a down payment on her dream home.

I thought about the impact we could have if we suggested that we run the program again, the financial return on securing another partnership with them, and the credibility it would lend to the Manifest brand to have a second corporate partnership with this amazing partner. At the same time, I thought about how exhausted both Tasha and I were running the series for eight weeks in a row with Tasha commuting up every weekend. I knew that even though I so badly wanted to ask to run another series with this partner, it was not the time to do so and it would absolutely deplete us and potentially crumble Manifest.

So instead of launching into a second partnership, which we both wanted but knew was not realistic, we decided to take a month off to rest, recalibrate, and talk about how we would continue to evolve Manifest's offerings going forward.

It was during this time that I realized this was a practice of self-love.

At this critical juncture in Manifest history, self-love for me was letting myself disrupt the idea that we *should* do the second series and that we *should* have taken it on because of the financial opportunity and brand equity it would create for Manifest.

At this critical juncture, self-love was confidently setting a boundary to protect our growing business from what we wanted (the second series in the partnership) and for what we wanted even more (a growing business we could sustain while also working full-time). While we survived the first series, we knew our current jobs and a second series could not coexist, so we opted out gracefully and honestly, leaving the door open for a future partnership at the point when we did have the capacity to take it on.

At this critical juncture, self-love was believing we had created something that was massively impactful and that because of this, even though we wouldn't be moving this partnership forward now, it wasn't the last time we would have an opportunity like this.

It was choosing abundance over scarcity. It was choosing to make this decision from a place of confidence and abundance, knowing our worth and potential, and doing what was *right* over choosing to make a decision based on the idea that opportunities like this were scarce and if we didn't take it now, we would never get the chance again.

Was it painful to turn down the opportunity? Yes!

Would it have been more painful to ruin what I know in the future will be an even more successful partnership because we had shifted into operating from a place of scarcity and did not have the right structure in place to support the partnership? Yes.

Do I feel like we made the *right* choice despite the pain we felt in the near term? Absolutely.

And how do I know this? Because after we took our break, we came back stronger and more confident than ever in our offerings, and we closed the year out with two of our biggest events and three more tables of ManifestHers.

YOU ARE THE ONLY PERSON WHO DECIDES WHAT SUCCESS LOOKS LIKE FOR YOU

> If I am always comparing myself to others, I will forever be at war with myself. And who needs that?
>
> —**Khloé Kardashian**, *Strong Looks Better Naked*

When you are on the path to your potential, regardless of your pace, there will be times where you feel like someone just sprinted past you, leaving you in the dust. This will cause you to question yourself and compare yourself to that person, and the comparison has to stop.

You are the only person who decides what success looks like for you. Remember this journey you are on is not a sprint; it is a marathon. You have to monitor and manage the amount of energy you have going out against what you've provisioned for the health, welfare, maintenance, and protection of your own essential being.

There will be times when you have what you need to sprint toward your summit, but when you are out of breath, your muscles are aching, and you feel like you are about to metaphorically pass out, you need to listen to your body and respond by giving it the space and grace it needs to recover.

When you compare yourself to others and ignore what your body is telling you and push yourself beyond your limits, the result is injury. Injuries kill momentum and leave you feeling stuck.

When you give yourself grace and space to listen to your body, mind, and heart and give yourself permission, truly practicing self-love and self-care, it is in this space that you can choose to recalibrate what your definition of success is. It is in this space that you can see where you've diverged from your true path and get back to it. It is in this space that you can choose the sustainable pace at which you want to pursue your goals and fulfill your purpose and potential.

WHAT I DID

When I started *really* practicing self-love and self-care under the new ManifestHer definitions, I had to constantly remind myself that I was the only person who could define success for me and that any time I had a thought about what I *"should"* be doing, that was an unnecessary and unhealthy comparison that I had manufactured for myself.

I started being more deliberate about choosing what was necessary for my health and welfare while in pursuit of my goals.

I relinquished myself from feeling ashamed for needing to recalibrate how fast and how aggressive I was willing to move toward goals for Manifest while balancing my full-time job, which had started to bring more meaning into my life again. In fact, the work I was doing at Manifest had informed my passions at the office—so much so that I advocated for and was promoted to help lead our company in building our very first brand community, sparking a new flame for me in my day-to-day.

I decided not to be ashamed when the visions and goals we were sprinting toward changed and evolved. Instead, I shared them with Tasha and the rest of the Manifest team and the reasons why they were changing and evolving. I used the goal-setting tools to recalibrate our course.

I chose to express deep affection for my essential being by continuing to take time to provision what was necessary for my health and welfare by keeping up my daily yoga practice and reading while also making moves with Manifest and at work and letting other parts of my life fade in and out as there was space for them.

My *Challenge* for You

How can you embrace these new definitions of self-love and self-care in your life?
Where do you have opportunities to grow your practice of self-love under the new definition?
Where do you have opportunities to grow your practice of self-care under the new definition?

Suggested *Reading*

Strong Looks Better Naked by Khloe Kardashian
Thrive: The Third Metric to Redefining Success and Creating a Life of Well-Being, Wisdom, and Wonder by Arianna Huffington

A *Song* to Remind You to Love on Yourself

"Good as Hell" by Lizzo

Notes

Step 10

DON'T GO IT ALONE—CREATE SPACE AT THE TABLE FOR PEOPLE WHO LIFT YOU UP

We are all community-made.
—Stef Caldwell

YES, I JUST QUOTED MYSELF, because after all the books I've ever read, not a single one has tackled this topic in the way I intend to do in this chapter.

There's something going on in the world right now where we've popularized the idea of being self-made to the point of ad nauseam. From every Instagram post to every *girl-boss* book online and in stores, everyone wants to be self-made.

Um . . . Why?

Why aren't we celebrating the fact that NONE of us are self-made, and I mean none of us.

But we ARE all community-made.

By virtue of the fact that we are brought into this world through the actions of two humans, who were the result of the actions of four other humans, we are inherently community-made, and I think it's time we start taking more pride in that!

If there is one person on this planet who believes this just as much as I do, it is Lori Harder, who literally wrote the book on building a tribe of like-minded women by providing the tools you need to authentically connect with existing and new friends and create the most powerful relationships you can possibly imagine.

BUILDING YOUR BLISS TRIBE

> You have to build a tribe that's either in support of the next level, or already at the next level.
> —**Lori Harder**, *A Tribe Called Bliss: Break Through Superficial Friendships, Create Real Connections, Reach Your Highest Potential*

As you continue the pursuit of your goals on the path to realizing your potential, you will most likely find that the amount of time you have to spend with others gets smaller, and because of this, you will notice that your circle gets smaller as well. It's only natural because relationships take time, and the more limited time you have, the less you'll have to give to these relationships. You will start to feel three equal and different forces pull on your relationships:

One force is going to be a magnet for authentic connection with the people you already have in your life. You will find yourself opening up to them more and more about the changes you are making in your life, and they will celebrate you for being 100 percent authentically yourself. These tried and true friendships are ones that you should continue to lean into; it's these people who have been and always will be there to back you up.

The second force is going to pull you in the direction of new relationships with people who possess the energy you know you need to continue moving in this new direction. You will find yourself creating authentic and powerful relationships with these new people so you can continue on your journey to realizing your potential. These new, blooming relationships are gifts for you from the universe. They are here to teach you new things and give you new experiences, and while you will have to nurture them (and some won't pan out exactly the way you think they will), they are here for you to learn from.

The third force is one that is going to be pushing you away from relationships that you were keeping around for convenience's sake or because you feared that if you lost those relationships, you would not find new ones. Because this new version of you calls for next-level relationships, it is only natural that the more you evolve and grow, the more you are going to outgrow some of the relationships you've been holding onto for too long, and that's okay. Saying goodbye to these relationships may be painful or scary at first, but remember when you clear space in your life, you invite new energy in, and the new energy that is coming to you in the form of new relationships is something so worthy of creating space for.

SAY GOODBYE TO FRIENDSHIPS NO LONGER SERVING YOU

"How do you know when it's time to say goodbye to relationships that are no longer serving you?" ManifestHers ask me all the time.

In Stephen Covey's book *The 7 Habits of Highly Effective People: Powerful Lessons in Personal Change*, he suggests that relationships are like bank accounts: you make deposits and withdrawals in accounts between two parties for your entire life. The pockets of some of your relationships are so deep and so full they could buy you a penthouse suite in a high-rise in Chicago with a souped-up sports car to go with it, but there are others that have your pockets so empty you would be left sleeping on the street in the dead of winter.

You can measure the balance of the emotional bank account between you and your friends by taking the sum of love and trust and positive experiences you feel toward another person and subtracting the negative experiences or betrayals you've had with that person. Over time, a positive relationship builds a strong account balance and minor hiccups along the way do little to impact the status of the relationship.

On the other hand, even a positive relationship with a strong balance can be depleted quickly under the right circumstances. A strong negative experience, constant and consistent discourtesies, or worse, betrayals of trust—these can all cause big hits to the balances between friends.

Covey suggests that when you think about your relationships, there are people *you just know* you have a very strong emotional bank account with. On the other hand, there are others who *you just know* you don't because spending time with them makes you feel icky, depleted, agitated, or worse.

And it's in these relationships that you need to ask yourself why you are in it in the first place. Does this relationship bring you joy? If not, why are you still holding onto it?

In Marie Kondo's book *The Life Changing Art of Tidying Up: The Japanese Art of Decluttering and Organizing,* a book about how to keep your home tidy, she suggests that people should "Keep only those things that speak to your heart. Then take the plunge and discard all the rest. By doing this, you can reset your life and embark on a new lifestyle."

Her recommended approach to doing so is to put everything you own in your world out in the open and then pick up each item, one at a time, and ask yourself, "Does this bring me joy?"

If the item does indeed bring you joy, you get to keep it, and it goes back to its place where you appreciate it and allow it to create joy for you. If the item does not bring you joy, then you have to discard the item; it has served its wonderful purpose and now it no longer does, and the two of you can part.

When Marie tells her clients that they have to discard something, she reminds them, "It is human nature to resist throwing something away, even when we know that we should," but at the same time, "the process of assessing how you feel about the things you own, identifying those that have fulfilled their purpose, expressing your gratitude and bidding them farewell, is really about examining your inner self, a rite of passage to a new life."

Just as you do this for the things in your home, I think you need to do the same thing for your relationships!

Everyone is community-made and, just as with things, there are people who come in and out of your life for a reason. Some are meant to be the main characters on your journey and stand by you and support you along the way, while others are meant to be background characters—they serve a purpose, they teach you something about yourself or about the world, and then they are meant to fade away.

It's the relationships that you hold onto under false pretenses, assuming they are meant to be main characters with you on your journey when in actuality they are meant to be background characters, that cause you pain. But when you evaluate them objectively and then start to view them as having fulfilled their purpose, you can say thank you to them and set them free to find new purpose, providing not just a rite of passage for you to a new life but a rite of passage for them as well.

In Kondo's book, she suggests that the first option for things that do not bring you joy is truly discarding the item, saying goodbye, and letting the item go on to fulfill its purpose in the great circle of life.

The second is donating the item to a place that will provide it to someone who seeks it out, someone who wants it or needs it, someone who will appreciate the item when it comes to them.

The final is selling the item—literally sharing the item with someone who will appreciate it as if it were brand new.

But the two things you cannot do with the discard pile is 1) keep it or 2) pawn it off on an unsuspecting friend.

Now this is a great list of things to do when you Kon-Marie your house, but it feels a little harsh for when you Kon-Marie your friendships. This is why I want to share a tool I picked up along the way that has helped me productively say goodbye to relationships that were not bringing me joy.

This method is called radical candor.

USE RADICAL CANDOR TO SAY GOODBYE TO THOSE WHO DO NOT BRING YOU JOY

Radical candor is a communication framework designed by Kim Scott, a former Googler and total badass. Her mission is to disrupt the way we communicate with one another at work by bringing our humanity back into the workplace.

We've adopted this communication style on the Manifest team and at my full-time job. Not only is it effective but it makes my life and my relationships more enjoyable and authentic.

That said, I've found that radical candor's applicability extends far beyond the workforce, so I am really excited to share it with you so you too can unlock next-order relationships in your life.

Radical candor is one of four communication styles that you can employ to have conversations with others. Radical candor suggests that when you communicate with others, you should both care personally and challenge directly. This style of communication is what everyone would prefer to be on the receiving end of but it is rarely employed because of its counterparts, ruinous empathy, obnoxious aggression, and manipulative insincerity, which actually come more naturally to people.

Radical candor is all about caring personally while challenging directly, whereas ruinous empathy sits in the camp of caring personally while not actually challenging, obnoxious aggression is when you don't show that you care and you challenge directly, and manipulative insincerity is what happens when you don't actually care and you also don't challenge.

While radical candor has the potential to uplift others and challenge them to be their best selves, the other types of communication can leave others feeling used, depleted, or, honestly, frustrated, attacked, or detached.

What I love about radical candor is that it works for both healthy relationships that you want to make healthier and for the relationships that are no longer bringing you joy that you need to let go of entirely or for the time being.

I know because I've done it, and while it wasn't easy having tough conversations with friends who were no longer bringing me joy, expressing gratitude for all the joy the relationship had brought set us both free to go on with our lives and in the end we both felt liberated by the mutual understanding that we no longer had to maintain our relationship—it had simply run its course.

RADICAL CANDOR IN PRACTICE

One of my dearest friends in the world is a woman who took me in at a time in college when I was not getting along with a roommate and who let me sleep on her couch, almost exclusively, for an entire year. Let's call her Alex.

Alex and I played rugby together, we watched movies together, we did homework together, we pushed each other on our beliefs and discovered many things about ourselves together. Alex was one of the first best friends I ever had. I truly felt indebted to her after my year of couch surfing. She was a tremendous friend.

When we graduated college, we lived in different states; I moved to Chicago and she moved out west. The more I got into my career and my relationships in Chicago, the more she got into her higher education and her relationships out west. The physical distance and the psychological distance of the different life stages we were entering put strain on our relationship.

I called less and less, and this hurt her. I was really enjoying my life and career in Chicago, and she was having some trouble assimilating out west, and this hurt her. It got to the point that when we did talk, she complained a lot. I didn't know how to tell her that I didn't want to hear her complaints anymore, so my calls got less frequent, and this hurt her even more.

Regardless, when Ronnie proposed, she was one of the first people I called. I couldn't wait to ask her to be my co-maid of honor!

She was ecstatic for us and graciously accepted the position.

But when it came time to show up for me on the wedding day, she just didn't show up in the way I wanted and needed her to. Her actions felt deliberately selfish and I was truly hurt. I was so hurt that I couldn't bear talking to her, so I chose to simply ignore her on our special day.

The next day, I woke up feeling like our emotional bank account was completely depleted. I had to ask myself, after what transpired the night before, does this relationship still bring me joy? The answer was no.

I toiled for weeks over the decision to talk to her. I mean, she was my best friend—I told this woman everything! We had so much fun together, and she was into the same things as me. How could I tell her this? It would devastate her. I was devastated thinking about it, but at the same time, I couldn't hold onto this relationship any longer. It just wasn't bringing me joy, and it was taking up space, clouding my mind, and weighing on my conscience.

Finally, I got up the nerve to tell her how I was feeling and that the next time she was in town, I wanted to have a conversation with her.

When the day came, I was nervous, my palms were sweaty, and emotions were high on both sides. We broke up. She cried, I cried, but ultimately, we both felt the closure we needed to move into the next phase of our relationship.

"Alex, you have been one of my best friends for a very long time, and I am eternally grateful for everything that our relationship has given to me. I truly would not be the same person now if it hadn't been for you in my life. Your actions and your words on my wedding day were unacceptable. They were hurtful, and as much as I'd like to be, I'm not over it, and I need time to heal. While I am healing, I can't have you around. I love you and I appreciate you and I want the best for you. I want the best for me, too, and right now, that means I need space."

At the end of the conversation, we hugged and then we parted ways. In the age of social media and unlimited access to communication, we do touch base on and off, but there is a clear boundary now that protects my heart and protects hers.

If I could go back in time, I wish I would have known about radical candor earlier. I wish I would have been braver to have a more candid conversation earlier, and I do wonder whether the outcome would have been different, but I am still grateful for the lesson this experience taught me. And I am grateful for the communication tool to continue to prune my relationships and continuously build better relationships with others going forward.

Radical candor is important for all of your friendships: friendships you need to let go of, friendships you need to space from, friendships you want to invest in, and most importantly, the friendships that lift you up and help you get to the next level.

Trust me on this: for the ones you need to let go of, it will be hard, but it will be worth it. The space you will feel, the clarity of mind, and the pressure relief will only create space for more joy and bliss to enter.

USING ABUNDANCE TO HELP OLD AND NEW FRIENDSHIPS BLOOM

My other best friend and co-maid of honor is the captain of the history-making Team USA Women's Rugby Team, the first women's rugby team in history to play rugby at the Olympics. Among other admirable traits (she's smart, beautiful, and funny), she has a pretty incredible life, one that would make most people green with envy.

She played in the Olympics in 2016 in Rio de Janeiro, where she rubbed elbows with the world's most elite athletes, and upon her return, she was invited to the White House to meet Barack and Michelle Obama. Not only is her jet-setting lifestyle something of incredible grandeur but her body is literally out of a fitness magazine. A few years ago, in her small hometown, the mayor of the city honored her with a day in her name, Lauren Doyle Day.

So how is it that an "average Jane" like me can go about being friends with such a tremendously admirable person without having deep-rooted feelings of jealousy?

Well, I'd be lying to you if I said it was easy, and there was never a moment in my life when I wasn't both her best friend and jealous of her at the same time.

If you follow the Manifest team, then you know we love *The 15 Commitments of Conscious Leadership: A New Paradigm for Sustainable Success*. The book offers fifteen mantras for living a more meaningful life and being a better leader, one of which is "I commit to experiencing that I have enough of everything, including time, money, love, energy, space, resources, etc.," and these mantras helped me shift from feelings of jealousy to feelings of absolute love.

When I first entered college, I had a dysfunctional view of my friendships and the world around me. If any other person (specifically women) got more than I—or worse yet, what I wanted and couldn't get—then I would be in a fit of jealousy.

On move-in day, the day I first met Lauren, I sized her up and I envied her perfect body. In the weeks that followed, I took notice of the attention she received from boys, our coach, and our teammates due to her tremendous athleticism. It made me jealous because when I compared myself to her, I didn't stack up. I desperately wanted what she so easily was able to get.

But as the first semester of school went on, I got to know her on and off the field. We spent hours together at practice, in the weight room, over long breakfasts and dinners, and in the hours we lay in our separate twin beds in our dorm room. We talked to each other from our pillows, staring up at the ceiling, all the while getting to know each other on a deep level, laughing, gossiping, revealing our dreams and our fears. After a few months, we had quickly become best friends.

Maybe I'm alone here, but I don't think I'm the first to admit to being both best friends with someone and jealous of them at the same time. But how is that possible?

Here's what I learned: it's not.

Jealousy is the cousin of comparison, and comparison is the death of joy. Without joy, there is no room for love, and without absolute love, you cannot have friendship. More important, without loving yourself, you can never truly love another person.

I needed to fall in love with myself to truly be there for Lauren. At that point in time, falling in love with myself meant falling in love with my body (so I could stop comparing mine to hers). It also meant carving out a place on our team where I didn't have to compare myself to Lauren either, thus enabling me to love and support her and receive her love and support in return.

With the end of the school year approaching and the seniors on our team graduating, there were field positions open on the team. I knew exactly the one I wanted to carve out for myself:

one on defense, where I wouldn't be competing with Lauren—I would be protecting her. I needed to be better for her and for our team, and that meant I needed to be better for myself.

I trained for the entire summer between our freshman and sophomore year to get in the best shape of my life, so I could fall in love with myself and my body, I could get the field position I was vying for, and, in turn, be a better friend to Lauren on and off the field.

When I stopped focusing on comparing myself to her and instead focused on being there for her, we were both able to thrive.

That summer, I was successful in losing nearly thirty pounds and taking minutes off my mile time. The following season, Lauren and I took the field by storm and were awarded Most Valuable Player and Most Improved Player. To my surprise, the result of my weight loss journey didn't mean any of the energy Lauren received went away; it simply meant I was able to get the energy I desired too!

We were different, we were on our own unique paths, we were uniquely awesome at our own thing, and we were absolutely stronger when we were working together.

She and I could both be total badasses in our own right, and one of us having something didn't mean the other had to go without. We could both have it all.

USING ABUNDANCE TO ATTRACT HER ABUNDANCE

I don't think I am the first woman to admit to being jealous of her best friend. In fact, when I told Lauren this very story, she said to me, "That's hilarious because I was jealous of you. I thought you had such a wonderful personality and such great boobs!"

We both had a laugh. Why did we have to be jealous of each other? Why did we operate from a space of scarcity? Why do women do this to each other and to their friendships?

I've reflected on this a lot over the last year, and where I've netted out is that women are biologically hardwired for friendship but unfortunately, technology is outpacing evolution. While our biology is still capable of success in tribes and hunter-gatherer communities, we are finding ourselves in modern communities where the requirements that are thrust upon women to be a productive member of the tribe and community are vastly different than our humble hunter-gatherer roots.

In the book *Disrupt-Her: A Manifesto for the Modern Woman*, Miki Agarwal suggests modern feminism is marked by three major feminist movements: women's suffrage (late 1800s), in which women earned the right to vote; the gender equality in the workforce movement (1960s), through which women fought for nondiscrimination in the workforce; and finally the intersectional-feminist movement (1990s), which recognized members of the gay and trans community as part of the feminist movement.

All this progress is without a doubt positive and yet it in some ways has created a toxic environment in which women, who are biologically programmed for nurture and leaning on each other, have been reprogrammed out of societal necessity to adopt a more macho mentality, clawing tooth and nail for every job, every promotion, and every opportunity for more responsibility. It's as if we are all battling for a seat at the table because there are very few seats. Fewer than 5 percent of Fortune 500 CEOs today are women, and fewer than 6 percent of founders who receive funding from venture capitalists are women.

While some women have awakened to the power of numbers to advance our cause, others have focused solely on advancing their individual cause. This disparity has created a lack of trust among women, as it's difficult to know who you can trust and who might be sandbagging you to get ahead.

Ultimately, this ends up holding back our entire gender because we believe things like "Women are too catty," "Women are too competitive," "Women are intimidated by me," "It's hard to meet women and forge meaningful connections with them," and "I don't have time for female friends; they are energy vampires."

But what's so sad about these beliefs is none of us actually want to believe them. They make us feel icky about our relationships with other women, who we are biologically programmed to want to be around, but socially programmed to not trust because of our beliefs, and the experiences that corroborate them.

Think about it: depending on your age, we all grew up with deeply held beliefs about what it means to be a woman and to have women as friends. Those ideas were passed down to us by women in our lives—our mothers, our grandmothers, and other influential women (aunts, godparents, etc.).

The ideas that they held were diluted each time they were passed down, but we are still fighting a pretty uphill battle when it comes to our beliefs about our relationships with other women and our role as women in the world and in the workplace.

Take, for example, our grandmothers, who were born in the 1920s, on the heels of the women's suffrage movement. Or our mothers, who were born in the 1960s and '70s, in the wake of the first mass movement of women from the home to the workforce. We were born in the 1980s and '90s, about the same time that members of the LGBTQ community were starting to successfully reorient society to see sexuality on a scale that wasn't just binary and heterosexual—a belief that took more than two decades to make its way into a law that recognizes same-sex marriage as a type of legal relationship in America.

The point is, the world appears to be moving very fast right now because of technology. However, it takes a lot longer to change our minds and hearts than it does to change a feature on an iPhone, and reconstructing these deeply held beliefs of how things "should be" will take hard work, and decades of it, for us to see the fruits of our labor.

So what do we do about it?

My take, at least right now, is to start by building an abundance mindset.

According to Diana Chapman, Jim Dethmer, and Kaley Klemp in *The 15 Commitments of Conscious Leadership*, in abundance, we operate from a standpoint of "I commit to being the source of my security, control, and approval." We have agency over our lives and our decisions, and we are the deciders of our own happiness. In abundance, we "commit to living in appreciation, fully opening to both receiving and giving appreciation." In abundance, we "commit to seeing all people and circumstances as allies that are perfectly suited to help me learn the most important things for my growth."

Women who operate from a place of abundance have an incredible propensity to shatter outdated beliefs and glass ceilings for and with other women.

As you start to think about the space you created in your relationships from the previous section, and as you start to seek out new relationships and inspiring people you want to fill that space in your life, remember that you attract the energy you put into the universe.

If you are seeking a relationship with another woman who will genuinely celebrate your wins, you should find opportunities to genuinely celebrate hers. If you are seeking a friendship with another woman where you can be authentic and unapologetically yourself, give her the space to be authentic and unapologetically herself. If you are seeking a friendship where you can both care personally and challenge each other directly in an effort to uplift one another, tell your new friend about radical candor and then practice it with her!

Be the change you want to see in the world around you, and the world around you will change. Choose to operate from a space of abundance and agency and see how people show up differently in your life.

EEK—NEW RELATIONSHIPS, THAT SOUNDS TERRIFYING!

"Hi, I don't know if you remember me, but I'm Helena. We went to high school together, and I've been following everything you've been doing with Manifest, and I've been dying to reach out. I'd love to help in any way I can. Would you be interested in grabbing a coffee and telling me all about what you guys are doing?"

And just like that, my life changed.

Helena is one of the most commanding people I know, and she commanded the hell out of me when she slipped into my DMs (direct messages) on Instagram and completely rocked my world.

Someone cares about what Manifest is doing? I thought as I read her message over and over and over, dumbfounded and deciding what to write back.

"OMG! Hieeee!" My thumbs moved a mile a minute. "I would absolutely love to tell you more, and we could use any help we can get! What does next week look like for you?"

A week later, she walked into my life, and I'm truly convinced she is here to stay.

We sat down, did a coffee cheers, and she dug right in. "What have you been up to since high school?" she asked.

I responded.

"Wow, sounds like you work for a really cool company now," she said. "How did you end up with the idea for Manifest? Tell me more about Manifest."

"Wahhh-wahhh-wahhh-wahhh-wahhh," my phone alarm screamed.

I wasn't sure how the coffee date was going to go, so I'd set a timer on my phone for an hour so I could politely tell her I had to go home if the conversation was miserable.

But I wasn't miserable. She fired questions at me left and right, and we'd spent an hour talking about everything I'd been up to and everything Tasha and I were trying to accomplish with Manifest when the timer went off. I set the timer for another hour, when I really did have to go, and we spent another full hour connecting.

"Wahhh-wahhh-wahhh-wahhh-wahhh," my phone alarm screamed for the second time.

"Ugh, I am so bummed to cut you off, but I really have to go home," I whined, feeling my own disappointment bump up against hers.

"I'll drive you!" she said.

I accepted, and so began the story of our third Manifest partner.

Wow, that experience of connecting with Helena was truly unlike anything I've felt in a long time, I thought when I got home. *Why did that feel so different?*

And as I started to dissect our conversation and how everything since it has played out, it comes down to what I learned from Dale Carnegie.

> *"You can make more friends in two months by becoming interested in other people than you can in two years by trying to get other people interested in you."*
> —**Dale Carnegie**, *How to Win Friends and Influence People*

Helena and I showed up that day both genuinely and deeply interested in one another—and more than that, she had sincerely flattered me, and I her. There was immediate, mutual appreciation and a blooming new friendship.

"The difference between appreciation and flattery? That is simple. One is sincere and the other insincere. One comes from the heart out; the other from the teeth out. One is unselfish; the other selfish. One is universally admired; the other universally condemned."
—**Dale Carnegie,** *How to Win Friends and Influence People*

At Manifest, we've heard from countless women just how hard it is as an adult woman to meet others who you sincerely connect with. To this, we always share Dale Carnegie's sound advice: the best way to make friends is to get really interested in *them*.

Think about when you were a kid. How many times were you in the middle of playing chalk on the driveway or poking an inchworm with a stick when some other kid ran up to you and asked, "What are you doing? Why are you doing that? Can I play with you?" and you were instant friends.

As adults, we get it in our heads that the game is somehow harder, but it's not. We just get so self-conscious about being enough for the other person that instead of showing up from a place of genuine curiosity, interest, and a strong desire to get to know the other person—instead of just showing up as we are and letting that be enough—we show up from a space of insecurity and trying to prove that we fit in.

The key to making new, authentic, amazing friendships? Don't worry about being *interesting*. Be *interested*.

Who are you most curious about? Reach out to that person and, using radical candor and authentic appreciation, ask them to go out to coffee with you. If this makes you nervous, write down a list of questions you want to ask them.

If you don't A-S-K, you won't G-E-T. It is entirely possible that this person you are really excited to talk to is looking for exactly this kind of conversation or friendship, and you will never know that unless you A-S-K. Don't get too attached to whether or not they respond to your A-S-K or the outcome of the conversation. Remember to come from a place of abundance; if this conversation doesn't work out, there are a million more to be had out there in the universe!

ACTUALLY ENJOY MEETING NEW PEOPLE BY AVOIDING THE SHALLOW END

"Where do you live? What do you do? Oh, you aren't working right now?" Shit. Uh . . . *think, Stef, think!* "What shows are you into?"

I've been there. I'm sure you've been there. And we hate it! Hot damn, do we hate it!

Chances are that person you just reached out to at the end of the last section hates it too.

What is *it*? The shallow end.

And it's everywhere we go: Every networking event, every water cooler conversation. It's the conversations we have at the gym and on the train. It's everywhere. We're drowning in the shallow end of surface-level small talk, and none of us even want to be at that end of the pool.

When I picked up Lori Harder's *A Tribe Called Bliss*, I literally felt like she was speaking directly to me when she said, "You know what would really hit the spot? A soul-stirring conversation and an authentic connection. Tell me, what is your soul screaming at you to do and what can't you die without doing? C'mon, I'm not alone in this feeling, am I?"

No, Lori, you are not alone. You are so not alone.

More than anything else, the thing that plagues new adult friendships (and to some extent, existing friendships), especially between women, is this false belief that we have to stick to the shallow end for fear of social rejection if we don't!

But, let me ask you this: *Is it working?*

Maybe I'm alone, but I'll be the first to raise my hand and say, "NO! It's not, and it's miserable!" And I go to these events hoping that finally it will be different and when it's not, I come home deflated again, complaining to Ronnie about how horrible all these events actually are and how freaking hard it is to meet new friends as an adult.

Like Katniss, I think there are women around the world who are standing up and saying, "It's not working, I want to make it better, and I VOLUNTEER AS TRIBUTE!"

> How we're attempting to connect and communicate woman-to-woman is working about as well as searching for fudge brownies in a steaming cow pie. There are definitely goddesses waiting to elevate with you, as you are already learning, but unchecked emotions, lack of boundaries, fear of rejection, and need for acceptance are turning how we communicate into a shit show. It just all feels so messy and complicated, but it doesn't have to be that way.
>
> **—Lori Harder**

THE ANTIDOTE? AUTHENTICITY. VULNERABILITY. BETTER QUESTIONS.

So, you locked in lunch with your dream girl. You were so nervous to reach out to her, but she's agreed to go to coffee with you, and you can't freaking wait. A new relationship with so much potential to bloom!

You have a million things you want to ask her, but how are you going to get there? You are not going to get there wading through the shallow end. It would be totally unnatural to say, "OMG! I love those earrings. Where did you get them? And also, while you are answering that question, could you tell me how you developed such an incredible amount of confidence, and um, also, do you ever get uh, gulp, uh, do you ever wake up afraid that you are standing at the trailhead of your potential and won't ever be able to take a single step forward?"

Nope, it doesn't generally work out like that. Fortunately, there are a few things you can do to guarantee a soul-stirring conversation.

Be Authentic and Appreciative

General rule of thumb: People love people who love them.

Instead of starting the conversation by asking what neighborhood this badass lives in, start the conversation by telling her why you actually wanted to start the conversation in the first place.

If you reached out and you are meeting up: "I reached out to you because I am truly impressed by all that you've managed to accomplish. I am so inspired by your journey, and I thought it would be really great to sit down with someone whom I admire so much to learn about your path."

If you are at a networking event: "I came over because I noticed how you just seem to be a magnet for people. I try to surround myself with people like you, and so I just had to know your story."

Be Vulnerable

I guarantee you this will be uncomfortable the first time you do it, which is why you should let this person know you are feeling uncomfortable! It's okay to feel uncomfortable about it. Think about it: we've basically been training our entire lives not to do this stuff! Be real about it.

If you reached out and you are meeting up: "Honestly, I feel like I am super awkward when it comes to this sort of thing, but I'm trying to broaden my horizons by meeting new people and being really thoughtful about who I reach out to. I am seeking more meaningful connections with people these days, so I hope I don't come off as too forward or anything like that. I'm a little nervous, for whatever reason, and I figured I would just tell you so you know where I'm coming from."

If you are at a networking event: "I hate these types of events. I always feel so socially awkward and don't really know how to navigate the room. I get kind of shy when I'm in a big room of strangers. You looked like a person I really wanted to get to know, so I figured I would come over. I hope that's not too forward. I'm kind of new to this style of networking, but maybe you are in the same boat and hate this too."

Ask Better Questions

You've broken the ice and you've shown up authentically appreciative and shared your vulnerability. You have now lit the path for your conversation partner to reciprocate the vulnerability and have a truly wonderful conversation.

Remember my advice from the last section: when you want to make friends, it's not about being interesting; it's about being interested. Below is a list of amazing questions you could use to get the conversation flowing.

Most people would probably ask where you are from and what you do for a living, but I'd rather know:

"What are you most excited about in life right now? What are you most proud of? What are you most nervous about or what scares you the most? Where are you struggling the most? What would you say are your biggest strengths? Where are you getting the most fulfillment from in your life? What's draining you the most? What's missing in your life right now? Do you have any secret passions you want to pursue?" (Lori Harder, *A Tribe Called Bliss*)

And remember, once the conversation is flowing, keep it flowing by continuing to be interested!

It doesn't matter where it goes, or how it goes. The more you do this, the more you will naturally find rhythm and camaraderie with like-minded women. And when you find those women, you will truly enjoy the conversation and the company—and hey, you might even want to ask for her number when you are done!

WHAT I DID

I started using Radical Candor in all of my relationships. I started showing up for myself and for my relationships from a place of abundance. I started truly believing that I was the source of my own security, control, and approval.

I started to see all people and circumstances as allies perfectly suited to help me learn the most important things for my growth. I decided to believe that regardless of how any conversation turned out, I would experience growth from it.

I started A-S-King the people I admired most to have the conversations with me that I wanted to have with them. Even when it was uncomfortable or I felt vulnerable doing so, I constantly reminded myself that if you don't A-S-K, you won't G-E-T. There were some women who responded with a "HELL YES," and there were others who never responded at all.

I stopped putting pressure on myself and my conversational counterparts to have certain outcomes. I started entering all conversations believing that there were always more conversations to be had and more growth to be had, even if the one I was entering into didn't work out.

My *Challenge* for You

What relationships do you have in your life right now that you need to let go of? What opportunities do you have to leverage radical candor to say goodbye to them?

What relationships do you have in your life right now that you'd like to invest even more into? What opportunities do you have to move from a place of abundance and use radical candor to make even better?

What new relationships are you interested in pursuing right now? What opportunities do you have to reach out to those people and use radical candor and some of the questions provided in the chapter to authentically connect with them and get to know them?

Remember, if you don't A-S-K, you won't G-E-T.

Suggested *Reading*

How to Win Friends and Influence People by Dale Carnegie

A *Song* to Get You Pumped to Meet Some **Badass Friends**

"Where My Girls At?" by 702

Notes

_____

_____

_____

_____

_____

_____

_____

_____

_____

_____

_____

_____

_____

_____

_____

_____

_____

_____

Step 11

ENJOY THE JOURNEY; BE GRATEFUL FOR EVERY SINGLE DAY; WHEN THE UNIVERSE OPENS A DOOR, WALK THROUGH IT; DON'T EVER STOP MOVING FORWARD; AND DON'T FORGET TO LAUGH

We may not be able to witness our own eulogy, but we're actually writing it all the time, every day.
—Arianna Huffington, *Thrive: The Third Metric to Redefining Success and Creating a Life of Well-Being, Wisdom, and Wonder*

ANDREA, A DEAR FRIEND AND MANIFESTHER, once said to me, "I struggle to balance my ambition and my dreams for the future with contentment for where I am," and her words rocked me to my core.

I had been struggling with the same thing my entire life, even throughout the journey of writing this book. At every step along my path, every major life milestone, by the time I had hit the milestone, I was already thinking about the next one—it started in middle school. I couldn't wait to be in high school, then I couldn't wait to graduate college and move to the city, then I couldn't wait to live with my boyfriend, then I couldn't wait for my boyfriend to propose, then I couldn't wait to get married, and now I'm thinking about what it would be like to be a mom! I'm still struggling with this; even now, I am thinking about the next book I want to write, the podcast we are launching, the next stage in Manifest's existence.

There's always a milestone on the horizon, and there will always be a milestone on the horizon. The challenge isn't actually getting there—as you are hopefully feeling right now, getting there is very much in your control, as long as you know where you want to go (by setting your goals) and you put in the effort to get there (by focusing on your systems and process and being willing every single day to take one step forward). The challenge is staying present, grateful, and joyful on the journey.

ENJOY THE JOURNEY AND BE GRATEFUL FOR EVERY SINGLE DAY

I never felt Andrea's words more than just a few months ago when I received a phone call from a friend who told me one of our dearest ManifestHers had tragically passed away at the age of twenty-one.

When you build a community of women who come together with the sole purpose of getting to know one another and helping one another manifest their biggest dreams, you never think one of them with the biggest dreams won't make it to her next birthday.

Our angel, this ManifestHer, dreamt of saving enough money to buy her grandmother's home so she could support her in old age. She dreamt of having enough wealth to take care of all of her parents' financial needs. In her own words, she dreamt "To really LIVE my life on my own terms and to feel like I am in control of my life, whether it be my health, confidence, finances, travel, etc. I want to be able to travel to Paris on a drop of a dime, be able to abundantly tip my waitress for no reason without having to worry whether I'll be able to pay my bills now, donate generously to charities, treat my family and friends to the things they've been working their asses off their whole life to be able to do but never got there. I don't want to settle in any aspect of my life ever again—relationships, finances, or health wise. I'm not afraid to admit that I want it all, even if it may sound selfish."

When we danced with her at the end of the day and celebrated the woman she was going to Manifest, her ManifestHer, she danced to "Born This Way" by Lady Gaga, and we read this for her:

"She's living proof that there's nothing wrong with loving who you are, 'cause He made you perfectly. Abundance. Passion. Inspiration. This woman's ability to dismiss fear and move with confidence and authority is unbeatable. Even Lady Gaga has acknowledged her ability to bypass ALL the haters, stand up for minorities, and celebrate the outcasts, giving them a home and a safe place. Every day, she proves that hard work, dedication, goal setting, and goal slaying are in everyone's wheelhouse, if you want it badly enough. She built a wellness empire that enabled her to support everyone in her family, her grandmother and parents included. She's now a full-time traveler, exploring and uplifting people around the world by bringing her beautiful soul into every corner of the earth. It's an honor to know her. Put your hands together for this beautiful soul!"

Her passing shook me to my core and reminded me that life is incredibly fragile and nothing is guaranteed. As much as we have big visions for life and huge futures we want to manifest, it is just as important to be present and to be grateful and to cherish every single moment we have on this earth because the next moment is never a guarantee.

It's possible that she was and is Manifest's biggest supporter. She was one of the first to read this manuscript, she was one of the first to join our digital app, she was one of the first to RSVP for our first ever ManifestSoul program, and she told all of her friends and family about us.

The week of her passing, she and I were texting back and forth, and she was telling me how excited she was to come to our first ManifestSoul event and how our ManifestHer event had changed her life. In just a few short days, we would be reunited and I would get to wrap my arms around her and hear about all the exciting things she'd been working to manifest since leaving our table just a few months before.

The week that she passed was a hard week for us. Tasha was dealing with the death of another loved one, and navigating how we'd handle this ManifestHer's passing was uncharted territory for us.

I remember waking up in the morning after I'd received the news and going for a run to Lake Michigan, where I watched the sunrise and prayed for her and her family and prayed for an answer to how to navigate this difficult time graciously.

I've never been a very religious person, but I strongly believe that when our loved ones pass, they become our guardian angels. Whenever we are looking for inspiration or guidance, we can look to the sky and have a conversation with them through prayer and they, with their infinite wisdom, can help us by giving us ideas or sending us gifts when we need them. And these gifts come in the form of doors they open for us, show us, and tell us to walk through.

My grandfathers both passed away when I was younger, and so when I pray, I pray to them.

That morning, gazing at the sunrise over Lake Michigan, I prayed to my grandpas and asked that they greet our ManifestHer at the doors of heaven and make sure that she had everything she needed to have a wonderful time up there. While I was praying, two birds flew in from the corners of the sky and played together in front of me, swooping up and down and around, and I knew my grandpas were listening. I prayed that they send gifts and love to her family and that they would make sure her family was taken care of, since she would no longer be able to take care of them herself.

And then I prayed to our ManifestHer. I prayed that she had made a safe passage and that she knew this is what He wanted for her and that even if we didn't understand it now, there was something bigger in store for her upstairs. As I finished my prayer to her, a third bird swooped in from the corner of the sky and joined the other two as if they were old friends. "Hi, babe," I said to the third bird. "I'm glad you made it." She thanked me for my prayer and told me that He had brought her back to truly bring her beautiful soul into every corner of the earth. She told me not to worry, that she understood that this was all part of His master plan.

WHEN THE UNIVERSE OPENS A DOOR, WALK THROUGH IT

> The universe is always conspiring to support you, guide you, and compassionately lead you toward the highest good.
>
> —Gabby Bernstein, Super Attractor

The next day, I was on a walk with my mentor.

He had asked about the work I was doing with Manifest, and we talked about all the lives that had changed because of our programs. I told him about the manuscript I'd written and how the mission behind the book was to share with even more people our ideas and the tools that were helping us improve our lives and change the lives of our ManifestHers.

I mentioned that my intention was to shop the manuscript around for a year in hopes that a publishing house would pick it up and I wouldn't have to foot the bill for self-publishing. Out of nowhere, he suggested, "What if I gave you a gift for the amount you needed to self-publish the book?"

My heart shattered into a million pieces. This was the most generous offer I'd ever received. "Well, that would be an absolute dream come true," I said through tears.

"Why are you crying?" he asked.

And I told him how just the day before we'd lost our ManifestHer and that this blessing felt like it had been sent through him by a higher power. I was eternally grateful for the offering and graciously accepted it.

THE UNIVERSE HAS YOUR BACK

In my heart, I know for certain that the timing of this gift and the timing of our ManifestHer's passing was divine synchronicity and that the benevolent powers of the universe were on my side that day.

Since this moment, I've dived headfirst into the work of Gabby Bernstein, which has led me to seek more and more dialogue with my guardian angels than ever and encouraged me to constantly have conversations with our beloved late ManifestHer. I believe with complete certainty that she is with me, and I trust that together, her moving through me and with me, we can accomplish everything she sought to accomplish with her time on this earth.

Her divine presence reminds me to be ambitious and pursue my goals with the most intense tenacity; at the same time, she reminds me to be content, to be grateful, to be present in every moment that I am gifted, and to exist in joy.

It's not easy, and there are many moments where I forget our ManifestHer is with me and I shift out of joy—moments where the demands of the real world grind my gears and shift me away from being present and joyful for my time here—but I try very hard to be present and aware of this. When I feel myself shifting away, I call on our ManifestHer to help me get back into alignment.

DON'T EVER STOP MOVING FORWARD AND DON'T FORGET TO LAUGH

If you wait for certainty, you will spend your whole life standing still. And if you grow discouraged and give up when things get rough, you'll miss out on your best possible destiny. So the secret is to be excited about what is in your power to control, be accepting of what's not in your power to control, and then move with certainty into an uncertain future.

—**Kevin Hart**, *I Can't Make This Up: Life Lessons*

The last two years have been a wild ride filled with so much accomplishment and hard work, but despite all the amazing things that have happened on this journey, one of the best memories I have is sitting in the back of an Uber with Ronnie on our way from Newark airport to Manhattan, each of us with a single AirPod in one ear, listening to Kevin Hart's book on Audible and laughing so hard our sides were hurting and we were both crying big, chubby, happy tears out of both eyes.

We had spent all weekend with some friends in Upstate New York and arrived at Newark in time to hop our flight home. On arrival, we found out the flight had been delayed for more than six hours. As we watched it for the next twenty minutes, the delays were piling on, delay, delay, delay—at this rate, it would be two o'clock in the morning by the time we got back to Chicago.

> In life, you can choose to cry about the bullshit that happens to you or you can choose to laugh about it. I choose laughter.
> —**Kevin Hart,** *I Can't Make This Up: Life Lessons*

Standing there, suitcases in hand, we had to make a choice: sit at the airport and wait for the fate of our flight, hoping to get home, or cut our losses, change our flight to the next day, and embrace the gift of time to go explore New York City (one of our favorite cities) together with no plans, no commitments, and no expectations.

We chose the latter.

We spent the afternoon giggling like little kids to the stories in Kevin Hart's book as we gallivanted around Manhattan on foot, dodging rainstorms by diving into the closest bar and sipping whiskey as we went.

That night, we found ourselves at one of our favorite stand-up clubs in the city, where we saw one of the funniest stand-up sets of our lives.

And when we got back from the club, we snuggled, we smooched, and we fell more in love with each other than we'd ever been in our nearly decade of being together.

IT'S YOUR CHOICE

Everything in life is about the journey. There is no destination, and there will never be certainty. You can have the best plans in the world, you can have the tickets booked, suitcase packed, you can be at the airport, ready to board the flight to what you think is your final destination, and in the blink of an eye, it can all change. In that moment, you have a choice:

You can choose to be upset, get stuck, and wait for someone to choose your destiny for you.

or

You can choose to laugh, keep moving forward, enjoy the journey, and make your own destiny.

If you ever find yourself struggling to make the right choice, I encourage you to say a prayer to our ManifestHer, to call on her to guide you as she guides me and trust that she will be there helping you shift and realign in the same way she guides me.

My Final *Challenge* **for You**

How can you find more balance between your ambition and the future you are dreaming of and contentment for the journey you are on?

What doors has the universe opened for you that you need to walk through?

What opportunities do you have to choose to laugh and to keep moving forward?

What have you learned from this process?

What tools are you bringing with you on your journey from this point forward?

 Suggested *Reading*

I Can't Make This Up: Life Lessons by Kevin Hart and Neil Strauss

 A *Song* **for You on Your Journey**

"Born This Way" by Lady Gaga

Notes

_____
_____
_____
_____
_____
_____
_____
_____
_____
_____
_____
_____
_____
_____
_____
_____
_____
_____
_____
_____

Conclusion

I SEE YOU THERE, ManifestHer, walking the path, in hot pursuit of your potential and fulfilling your purpose.

You are ambitious. You are resourceful. You are a creative problem-solver. You have incredible drive and dedication. When you first started on this journey, you were stuck, you were scared to take steps forward, and you feared what it would feel like to live your entire life without knowing your purpose or leaving the trailhead of your potential. But now you have, and look at that—you are still alive to tell the story.

I promised you I would provide a practical, peer-to-peer guide from the perspective of someone who is in the thick of it with you, and you followed the guide to the end. Go you!

You disrupted the limiting beliefs you held about yourself by forgiving yourself, by creating healthy boundaries, and by expanding what you ever thought was possible in your life by curating a tribe of expanders who are validation that everything you want to manifest in your life is possible.

You revisited the dreams you had for your life for so long, finally brought structure to what those dreams are today, and created an action plan for achieving them.

And not only did you build the action plan, you actually took the action you needed to start achieving those goals on your list. You built momentum with your systems and you moved in pursuit of your passions, your potential, and your goals against Resistance.

You turned fear, failure, and shame into your compass and built even more confidence as you navigated through those emotions in the direction of your dreams.

And when the going got tough and you couldn't keep your original pace, you practiced self-love and self-care under the new, more productive definitions and kept moving forward anyway.

You've curated better, more healthy relationships in your life that are helping you take everything to the next level, and these relationships fill you with joy and catapult you in the direction of your ManifestHer.

But more than anything, you stayed humble, you learned to balance your ambition with contentment, and you started practicing gratitude for everything you are and everything you are becoming. You know that life is precious and life is fleeting, and you take time to appreciate life through gratitude and laughter.

I'm eternally grateful you picked up this book, and I hope I've fulfilled my promise to you to provide you with a curriculum that has empowered you to become unstuck and confidently navigate the ambiguity of your post-prescribed life through a lens of practicality.

But don't let the end of this book be the end of your journey to ManifestHer. Remember the plans we provided can get you through the next ten years if you let them and you follow them, but if there ever comes a time when they stop serving you, start back at square one. Forgive yourself for the fact that those goals aren't serving you, create boundaries and space for new goals to come to you, find expanders who resonate with you at that next life-stage, and let them be the anchor for your vision casting and goal setting. Remember setting and achieving your goals is a practice, and Resistance will always try to hold you back. When she shows up in your life, move with her; she is your guide to ManifestHer. Always use fear, failure, and shame as your compass and never forget to give yourself love.

Your life is sacred; the practice of manifesting your dream life is sacred. Create rituals of bringing your ManifestHer to life one day at a time.

Because who is she? She is the you that you were born to be.

You can, you will, you are, ManifestHer.

One Last *Book*

Super Attractor: Methods for Manifesting a Life beyond Your Wildest Dreams by Gabrielle Bernstein

One Last *Song*

"Higher" by DJ Khaled featuring Nipsey Hussle and John Legend

Acknowledgments

Thank you, Ronnie, for being the love of my life. I didn't fully comprehend what love, support, and partnership were until I met you. Thank you for letting me take over our one-bedroom apartment with my books and my thoughts throughout this process.

Thank you Tasha for being the reason why Manifest continues to exist. Without your dedication, support, love, and sweat, this book would have never come to life. Thank you Helena and Taylor for being part of our growing team of women committed to helping other women through our collective knowledge and networks.

Thank you to our beloved late ManifestHer for your eternal commitment to our growing community of women. We are grateful for your divine presence and guidance.

Thank you to the ManifestHers of our community for being part of this and giving us the grace of discovering Manifest while we are delivering it to you.

Thank you to the family I was born into, my parents, grand-mothers, brothers, and the family I've chosen, my in-laws (on both sides), the Commune, and all of my fabulously supportive friends for going out of their way to support and encourage our continued growth! Thank you to my grandfathers, may they rest in peace, for looking after my family and me as we blaze our paths in pursuit of our potential.

Thank you to the team at The Cadence Group for helping me bring this book to life!

Thank you to the folks at SimplyBe Agency for helping our team through the branding process.

And most importantly, thank you to my friend and mentor—you know who you are—for the gift of bringing this book to life. This would have never happened if it weren't for you and our walk through the park that day. You have given me the opportunity of a lifetime, and there is and will always be a special place for you in my heart.

About the Author

First of all, I'm honored that you decided to pick up this book. Of every book you could have selected from, I know you were meant to pick up and read this one, and I am so deeply grateful and giddy with excitement that you did. Somewhere in a kitchen, Tasha, Helena, Taylor, and I are doing a happy dance as we do any time another person joins our community.

When I went through the editing process with the incredible team at The Cadence Group, my editor suggested that I add an "About the Author" section at the end . . . Naturally, I went and selected all my favorite books off the bookshelves and read the About the Author sections at the end of their books. All were written in the third person, of course, and they were quite lovely.

But since I am sitting here, writing my own, I thought I would take it in a different direction. So here it goes:

I am deeply passionate about helping people and companies realize their potential. I have made my career by pioneering new roles at fast-growing technology companies. I thrive and drive massive impact in the most ambiguous of circumstances. I have no major awards to my name, I haven't been on any best-seller lists, I don't have a massive social media following, and I don't have my own TV show that I can tell you to watch that will rock your world or change your life—YET.

I don't know whether I will get the opportunity to speak at Fortune 500 companies or have my work be used by women around the world who will go on to be the biggest names in their industries with unbelievable success and wealth that they use to solve world hunger, and world peace, but I sure as hell hope I do.

What I do know is this:

I am manifesting a life that allows me to live my life on my own terms and to know I am in control, whether it be my relationships, my work, my health, my confidence, my finances, or anything else. I want to be able to say yes to anything at the drop of a hat, to be able to abundantly give money as a gift or an investment to those whose missions inspire me and who are people I believe in. I want to be able to donate generously to charities, to treat my family and friends to the things they've worked their asses off to achieve but haven't quite gotten there.

I want to change the lives of people around the world and help them realize their highest potential. I want to grow the world's most badass community of ManifestHers who never settle and constantly support one another through their collective knowledge and networks so we all rise together.

I'm not afraid to admit I want to be impactful, I want to have it all, and I want the exact same for every ManifestHer, present or future.

I hope that does an okay job for an "About the Author" section. ☺